# 100 IDEAS THAT CHANGED ADVERTISING

*Simon Veksner*

# 100 IDEAS THAT CHANGED ADVERTISING

*Simon Veksner*

Laurence King Publishing

# Introduction

There were two possible ways to write this book, because as well as the normal sense of 'idea', the word has an additional meaning in an advertising context. An 'advertising idea' is the concept behind a particular advertisement, and it would certainly have been possible to find 100 'advertising ideas' that changed advertising. For example, Apple's '1984' commercial initiated a new style of blockbuster 'event ad', and the Woodbury's soap 'A Skin you Love to Touch' campaign, which began in 1911, is generally held to be the first example of a sexual sell. But this approach would have fallen short, because not every idea that has changed advertising was an advertising idea. In fact, the vast majority of ideas that have changed advertising in a significant way have come from outside advertising.

Although advertising is not the world's oldest profession, it may well be the second oldest. Posters have been found perfectly preserved in the ruins of Pompeii, and the ancient Egyptians were known to have written ads on papyrus. But the growth of advertising has really tracked the growth of the industrial economy, with the first American ad agency only founded in 1842, and the business becoming a true force in society when the mass manufacture of consumer goods gave rise to a requirement for mass marketing. So the development of advertising as an industry has coincided with the most rapid period of change and development in human history – the period from the Industrial Revolution to today. It is not surprising, therefore, that the ad business has undergone enormous changes.

Since advertising is a service industry, a tool deployed by business, many of the changes that have affected advertising are changes in the business landscape. As business has become, first, international and then global, so has advertising. As business has become more efficient, more hi-tech and more professional, the business of advertising has too.

With the exception of certain political campaigns that may have influenced the result of an election, advertising does not change society. Instead it reflects society – which is why studying old ads is of such interest to social historians. Therefore the major changes that take place in society will, of necessity, influence advertising. The great sense of liberation that swept the world in the 1960s, for example, led to a liberation in the world of advertising; the industry's doors were flung open to every race, class and gender, and a new wave of creativity was unleashed.

That did not – and does not – necessarily mean 'true' creativity. Of course there is a great deal of 'art' involved in the crafting of a commercial. But as far as coming up with its own creative innovations, advertising must walk a delicate line. It is almost compulsory for an ad to offer up something new – a new joke, a new phrase or a new juxtaposition of imagery – if it is to attract and engage its audience. But fundamentally, advertising is a mass-market exercise, and needs to appeal to a mass audience. For that reason, advertising cannot run too far ahead of the popular taste; it is an enthusiastic co-opter rather than initiator of artistic styles. Artistic movements such as surrealism, for example, have had a huge influence on advertising, as have new developments in graphic design and web design.

Which brings us on to technology. Since advertising is a form of communication, advances in communications technology create new opportunities for advertising. The invention of the printing press led to print advertising, the invention of the radio very quickly created radio advertising, and likewise for TV, the internet and mobile phones. Every piece of technology costs money to operate, and every piece of technology (so far) has sought to monetize its users by serving them ads.

While acknowledging that the advertising business has been profoundly affected by changes in society and technology, it must also be recognized that there are instances in which the industry has changed itself. In fact the structure of a typical ad agency has altered significantly since its inception, with the evolution from pure media-buying operations to creators of advertising, and the addition of new roles such as account executives and account planners.

Over the years, ad agencies have also changed the way advertising is conducted by inventing new methods of selling, such as celebrity endorsements, comparative ads, product placement, and the use of jingles and slogans. The industry has also evolved new *theories* of selling, such as the 'unique selling proposition' (or USP) and the 'emotional selling proposition' (or ESP). Actually, in terms of theory, advertising has proved itself to be remarkably receptive to ideas from other sources, probably because – being such a competitive industry – any new idea that could possibly become a source of competitive advantage is enthusiastically adopted. Or at least given a try. In recent years, advertising has absorbed ideas from marketing (such as challenger-brand thinking), philosophy (semiotics), economics (behavioural economics) and even neuroscience (the application of neuroscientific theory to advertising research).

A chronological order seemed the most sensible way to organize all these various influences, though this book need not be read uni-directionally. Although some of the developments that changed advertising went on to open the door for others – for example, the growth of online advertising led directly to the proliferation of online branded games (or 'advergames') – each section is entirely self-contained.

Finally, even a casual dip or flick-through will reveal that this book is dominated by the story of American and British advertising. Although this may seem a little Anglo-Saxon-centric, any other approach would be hard to justify. The US is by far the world's largest advertising market, its size almost exceeding that of the other nine nations in the top ten combined. The US has also won more Cannes Lions for advertising than any other country (the UK is second). The vast majority of the world's leading agencies – including DDB, BBDO, BBH, Wieden+Kennedy, Grey, Y&R, Ogilvy & Mather, JWT, Lowe, McCann Erickson and Saatchi & Saatchi – were founded either by the British or the Americans. And the vast majority of the innovations in advertising – such as brainstorming, the tissue meeting and even TV advertising itself – were the products of either American or British minds. France's powerhouse agency, Publicis, makes that country a strong third player, but notwithstanding this, and the rise of China and India, the capital of world advertising is still New York, with London snapping at its heels.

This has not changed for over 100 years, and despite the myriad changes the industry has experienced in that time, it is perhaps worth making a point that is not noted anywhere else in a book that is about change: the fundamentals of advertising itself have *not* changed. Whether an advertising message is delivered via a medium as ancient as the poster or as modern as a tweet, it remains essentially an appeal on behalf of a company for someone to buy its goods or services. And an ad that is based on a human truth, for a product that answers a human need, and which communicates in an entertaining, engaging or involving way, will be successful. Despite all the societal and technological changes, this is what advertising has always been, and always will be: an entreaty, whether crassly or artfully made; a unique cocktail of art and commerce. That is where its fascination lies.

# *It's a stick-up*

RIGHT: *'Poster you can play with' using a smartphone, by DDB Stockholm for McDonald's, 2011.*

BOTTOM LEFT: *Election poster painted on the wall of a tavern in Pompeii, AD 79.*

OPPOSITE: *Poster by Jules Chéret for the Moulin Rouge in Paris, 1898.*

IDEA № 1
## THE POSTER

Posters are the oldest form of advertising. The ancient Egyptians used papyrus to make posters; commercial and political posters were found on the walls in the ruins of Pompeii. And as roads and cities multiplied, the billboard business thrived. Even today, few media can match the poster for impact.

The word 'poster' probably derives from the wooden roadside posts to which early billboards were attached. Nowadays, a more correct term is 'outdoor media', applying to ads seen anywhere outside the home – not just on hoardings but also buses, trains, taxis, even airships.

Early examples were handpainted directly on to walls, and each example was unique. But the invention of the printing press in the fifteenth century enabled mass production of posters. By 1722, Daniel Defoe (author of *Robinson Crusoe*) was complaining that in London 'the Corners of Streets were plastered over with Doctors Bills'. By the 1870s, the invention of lithography had enabled the reproduction of brighter colours, and a golden era of posters began – particularly in France, with artists such as Jules Chéret and Henri de Toulouse-Lautrec producing vivid, exuberant billboards for the Folies Bergère and Moulin Rouge. Gradually, illustration was replaced by photography, although handpainted posters are still found today in less-developed markets.

Unlike media such as print or radio, which feel personal, the poster is very much a broadcast medium – a public shout. As such, the best posters are brash and bold, with either a knockout visual or a short, punchy headline. In terms of their effectiveness as an advertising medium, posters score highly for reach (a wide range of people see them) and frequency (those people see them often – perhaps every day). They are less efficient at targeting specific groups.

Although it is the oldest of all media, the poster is anything but tired. In fact it has gained a new lease of life in recent years, thanks to new technology, such as scrolling posters, outdoor projections on the side of buildings and AR (augmented-reality) executions. In high-traffic locations such as Times Square and the London Underground, the traditional poster is being replaced by digital billboards, effectively becoming 'outdoor TV'. ∎

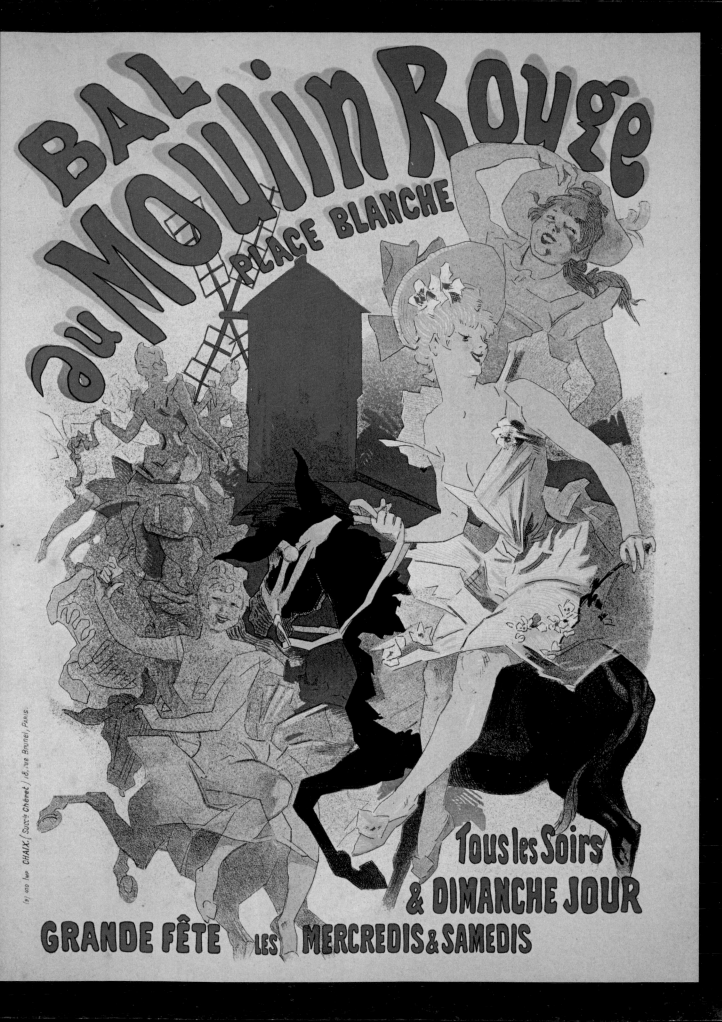

# For immediate uplift

RIGHT: Promotional fare on trips to London via Eurostar.

Londres est au coin de la rue

## IDEA № 2
# PROMOTIONS

Sales promotions are short-term incentives to purchase, the best known being the offer of a discount (e.g. '10 per cent off', '15 per cent off'), whose ultimate expression is the 'BOGO' or 'BOGOF' – 'Buy one get one free'.

The origins of the practice are unknown, but Roman taverns certainly created posters offering 'Two jugs of wine for the price of one'. Other than discounts, promotional tactics can include the offer of free samples, gifts with purchase, contests or cross-promotions, e.g. 'Free DVD rental when you buy a large pizza'. These strategies give marketers a whole new set of techniques to encourage consumers to choose their products over those of their competitors.

But sales promotions are not necessarily all aimed at the public. The store itself has a huge influence on what sells, so marketers frequently conduct 'trade' sales promotions, to encourage retailers to support their products. Examples include buy-back guarantees for unsold product, rewards for the best-performing sales staff, and eye-catching sales displays.

Of course it is impossible to tell in advance how successful a promotion will be – an unknown that has led to several notorious disasters. In 1992, Hoover offered British consumers free flights to America with every purchase of a vacuum cleaner over £100. They were overwhelmed with the demand and unable to deliver on their promise. The resulting court cases went on until 1998, cost Hoover almost £50 million, and ultimately led to the company being taken over.

In the US and the UK there is virtually no limit on how sales promotions can be run, but other markets are more restrictive. Germany has famously strict shopping laws, which specify the weeks in which sales may be held, limit the level of discount that may be offered outside those windows and place severe restrictions on give-aways. In one famous case, a baker was banned from giving a cloth bag to people buying more than ten rolls; in another, a garage was stopped from giving free car washes to repeat customers.

Sales promotions can have a fantastically successful short-term sales effect. However, if conducted too regularly, they end up training consumers to buy the product only when it is on special offer, making full-priced sales harder to achieve. They can also come across as gimmicky, so care must be taken that the tactic does not cheapen the brand's image. Some brands, such as Mercedes, almost never offer discounts or run contests. ∎

LEFT: A 2012 sales promotion for Dr Pepper offered consumers the chance to win either great prizes ... or pairs of underpants. It was the most successful on-pack promotion ever conducted by a Coca-Cola brand.

OPPOSITE: A newspaper promotion offering meals for £5.

# EAT OUT £5 from

To enjoy two courses of fine food from only £5 at more than a thousand restaurants across the UK, start collecting tokens in The Times and The Sunday Times today.

To get you started, here's your first token. Continue collecting throughout January.

You can find your nearest participating restaurant at

**thetimes.co.uk/eatout**

EAT OUT from £5
BONUS TOKEN
THE TIMES
THE SUNDAY TIMES

## THE TIMES
## THE SUNDAY TIMES

**Food you'll remember, at a price you'll never forget**

# Name recognition

IDEA Nº 3
# BRANDING

As the cities of the Middle Ages grew, tradesmen advertised their services by putting up signs – a cobbler would use a boot, and a blacksmith a horseshoe – since the general population could not read. These professional 'marks' evolved into brands, some of which are now worth billions of dollars.

Early brands that are still renowned today include Stella Artois (1366), Löwenbräu (1383) and Beretta firearms (1526). The purpose of the earliest brands – and a factor behind their ongoing importance – was identification. Brands help companies distinguish their products from the competition, and from generics. A sign of their value is that most companies are strenuous about protecting their brand names, slogans and distinctive graphic elements – going to court if necessary. Brands also act as a guarantee of quality. For example, a traveller seeing a bottle of Heineken for sale in a far-off country may be reassured that his beer will be of the same quality he is used to at home.

Another way to define a brand is as a collection of associations that exist in the mind of the consumer. A brand is everything that a person thinks or feels about a product, beyond their strict knowledge of its physical form. For example, a Volkswagen car is a real object made of steel, plastic and rubber. But the VW brand may stand for abstract qualities such as reliability, innovation and understated wit – qualities that are built and reinforced by its advertising.

Early brands were single-product brands, e.g. Tate & Lyle only sold syrup. But another advantage of brands is their ability to stretch across different (but related) product categories. In this way, a company such as Kellogg's saves a lot of money on marketing by being able to put their trusted brand name on a wide range of cereals, rather than needing to build trust afresh for each new product that they launch.

Another intriguing explanation for the enduring popularity of brands is that we find them useful as a means of saying something about ourselves. The brand we select – from the fashion logo we wear on a T-shirt, to the type of car we drive – acts as a kind of badge, signalling our values to other people. So although companies spend vast sums communicating their brand values to the public, it is interesting to note that brands themselves have become a form of communication. ∎

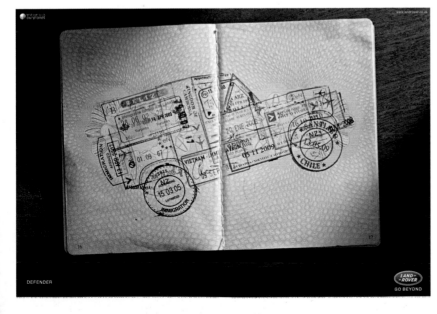

DEFENDER

LAND ROVER
GO BEYOND

OPPOSITE: An ad for what is currently the world's most valuable brand. So well known is its logo, the poster does not even need to mention the brand's name.

TOP RIGHT: Stella Artois ad. The brand's heritage can be traced back to 1366 when the Den Hoorn brewery was founded in Leuven, Belgium.

LEFT: Part of the success of the Land Rover brand lies in enabling the purchaser to 'signal' to others that they are 'an intrepid kind of person'.

# Hand-to-hand stuff

IDEA № 4
## THE LEAFLET

Towards the end of the Middle Ages, with more and more people able to read, and the cost of printing becoming cheaper, advertising expanded to include handbills. These evolved into the flyers and leaflets beloved of pizza-delivery companies that we see today.

ABOVE: *North Vietnamese propaganda – a leaflet offering a reward for GIs if they surrendered.*

BELOW: *Innovative informational leaflet advertising falconry in the UAE – it was designed to be folded up and delivered like a scroll.*

OPPOSITE: *Nightclub flyers are effective since they are left in the bars and clubs frequented by the target market. They reflect trends in contemporary music and culture; well-designed examples can become collectors' items.*

One of the first leaflets was a handbill printed by William Caxton in 1477 offering 'Pyes of Salisbury ... to any man spiritual or temporal to buy', although the ad referred to 'Pyes' in the sense of clerical rules, rather than meat-filled pastries. In the sixteenth and seventeenth centuries, handwritten bills known as 'siquis' were common in England. Originally these were used to advertise clerical positions; they earned their name because they were in Latin and usually began *si quis* (if anybody). But soon the notices took on various subjects including lost-and-found, and runaway apprentices.

Handbills had become a popular form of advertising by the early 1800s. They were handed out in the street or posted in town centres to catch the attention of passers-by, and advertised everything from hat-makers to evangelical religious groups.

The enduring success of flyers is due to their directness and immediacy – an ad thrust into a consumer's hand cannot be ignored, and they can be produced quickly and cheaply, especially since the introduction of inexpensive desktop publishing software in the 1990s. In recent years, the production of flyers via traditional printing services has largely migrated to the internet; customers submit their designs via email and receive a quantity of leaflets in the post.

The terms 'flyer' and 'leaflet' are more or less interchangeable. However, flyers are usually printed on 300gsm glossy card (110lb cover stock) and the printing may be low quality, whereas leaflets are slightly more reputable: lighter in weight but properly printed and may have folding pages. Both forms are handed out on the street, posted on bulletin boards in cafes and on university campuses, shoved through letter-boxes or given away at events. They can be a very effective type of direct marketing, and are especially useful for heavy targeting of tightly defined zones ... such as the delivery area of a local restaurant. ■

MOVEMENDOSA

25.04.2008 MOVEMENDOSA — INFERNO (NL)

# Selling off the page

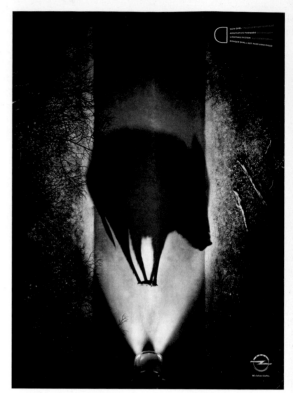

IDEA № 5
## PRESS ADVERTISING

In the seventeenth century, advertisements started to appear in weekly newspapers in England, promoting books and other newspapers to a newly literate population. The other important category, in disease-ravaged Europe, was medicines.

The first English-language newspaper was the *Weekly Newes* of London, first published in 1622. The first American newspaper to carry advertising was the *Boston News-Letter* in 1704 – its first ad offered a reward for the capture of a thief.

But early print ads were very different from advertisements today. Advertisers could make virtually any claims for their product, and frequently did, offering miracle cures via patent medicines. In appearance, ads were text-heavy and dull, by modern standards. They were rarely wider than a single column, and showed little innovation in terms of typefaces. James Gordon Bennett, publisher of the *New York Herald* from 1835 to 1867, introduced the innovation of ads that changed every day, just as the news did.

Before that, companies often ran the same ad for a year.

The Industrial Revolution created new categories of branded goods, ranging from soap to canned food to cigarettes, and newspapers grew on the back of the need to advertise these goods – in the US, the number of newspapers more than doubled between 1830 and 1860, increasing from 1,200 to 3,000. In 1899, N. W. Ayer launched the first million-dollar advertising campaign, for Uneeda Biscuit. In subsequent years the introduction of colour and improvements in paper and printing quality further improved the appeal of newspapers.

The success of newspapers as an advertising medium stems from their reasonable cost (per thousand people reached); short lead times – enabling flexibility and rapid response to events; and portability, which means they can be read while commuting, thus remaining in consumers' hands for up to an hour … in contrast to the mere seconds of dwell time afforded by a poster.

Print advertising was, for many years, the most important advertising medium, but as consumers have begun to go online for their news, the size of the market has declined – it was overtaken by television in 2010, and the internet in 2012. ∎

TO BE SOLD by William Yeomans, (in Charles Town Merchant,) a parcel of good Plantation Slaves. Encouragement will be given by taking Rice in Payment, or any Time Credit, Security to be given if required There's likewise to be sold, very good Troopling saddles and Furniture, choice Barbados and Boston Rum, also Cordial Waters and Limejuice, as well as a parcel of extraordinary Indian trading Goods, and many of other sorts suitable for the Season.

LATE NIGHT SPECIAL

# Evening Standard
### and St. James's Gazette

LARGER DAILY CIRCULATION THAN THAT OF UNDERLINE ANY TWO OTHER PENNY EVENING PAPERS.

No. 28,634.     LONDON, TUESDAY, APRIL 25, 1916.     ONE PENNY.

# NAVAL FIGHT OFF LOWESTOFT.

## RAID BY GERMAN BATTLE-CRUISER SQUADRON.

## LIGHT CRUISERS AND DESTROYERS

## ENEMY TACKLED BY BRITISH WARSHIPS AND CHASED BACK.

## THREE OF OUR VESSELS HIT.

The Secretary of the Admiralty makes the following announcement this afternoon:

**PRESS BUREAU, 1.40 p.m.**

About 4.30 this morning the German battle cruiser squadron, accompanied by light cruisers and destroyers, appeared off Lowestoft.

The local naval forces engaged it, and in about twenty minutes it returned to Germany, chased by our light cruisers and destroyers.

On shore two men, one woman, and a child were killed.

Material damage seems to have been insignificant.

So far as is known at present, two British light cruisers and a destroyer were hit, but none were sunk.

### PREVIOUS NAVAL RAIDS.

#### THE GREAT ATTACK ON YORKSHIRE COAST.

The first German naval raid in home waters took place on November 3, 1914, when early on the morning of that date a German squadron fired on the Halcyon, a coastguard gunboat engaged in patrolling. The Halcyon having reported the presence of these German warships, British warships shadowed them, but could not bring them to action before dusk. The rearmost German cruiser in retirement threw out mines, and Sub-

marine D5 was sunk by exploding one of these. This German squadron was seen from Yarmouth, upon which it fired, without damage except to the Halcyon.

#### Towns Bombarded.

A period of comparative inactivity followed, until, on December 16, 1914, the greatest attack made until the one now notified took place. For the first time for centuries the coast of England was directly and seriously attacked. German

warships appeared out of a fog near the shores of Yorkshire and Durham soon after daybreak and bombarded West Hartlepool, Scarborough, and Whitby. After remaining for about an hour on the coast they effected their escape to Germany. The loss of life among the civil population was considerable, and the wounded numerous. Churches, hospitals, and other public buildings were shelled.

At Hartlepool 55 persons were killed and 115 wounded; at Scarborough 23 were killed and 100 wounded; and at Whitby 19 were killed and 76 injured.

These totals were increased later owing to numerous deaths among the wounded to:—

| | |
|---|---|
| Killed | 127 |
| Wounded | 507 |

Included in these figures were:—

| | Killed. | Wounded. |
|---|---|---|
| Women | 39 | 133 |
| Children | 39 | 177 |

On this occasion all the known facts demonstrated that Germany had sent out all her effective battle cruisers. They were the Derfflinger, Seydlitz, Moltke, Von-der-Tann, and Blucher. The last has since been sunk, and the Moltke badly injured in the Baltic.

Before war began the rôle of the battle-cruiser was uncertain. Primarily intended to overhaul and destroy commerce-raiders, vessels of this class were for this reason faster than anything afloat, could keep the sea for long spells of time, and were provided with armaments which could overwhelm anything except Dreadnought battleships of the same period. Up till then—December 1914—nobody expected that battle-cruisers would be used to bombard defenceless towns and seaside places.

Presumably a similar squadron was in action in this latest raid.

A special article by our Naval Correspondent on the fight off Lowestoft appears on Page 2.

# REBELLION IN IRELAND.

## DUBLIN RIOTERS FORCIBLY SEIZE THE POST OFFICE.

## "IN POSSESSION OF PARTS OF CITY."

## TWELVE LIVES LOST: TROOPS FROM THE CURRAGH TO RESTORE ORDER.

In the House of Commons this afternoon,

Replying to Captain Craig, Mr. Birrell said grave disturbances had broken out in Dublin.

The Post Office had been forcibly taken, and twelve lives lost.

Telegraphic communication had been cut off, but the situation was well in hand.

The rebels were in possession of four or five different parts of the city.

The Press Bureau this afternoon announced that Sir Roger Casement, whose vain attempts to suborn Irish prisoners in Germany have been followed by his participation in an abortive scheme to land arms in Ireland, is now in London, awaiting trial for high treason.

### MR. BIRRELL'S NEWS.

#### SOLDIERS FROM THE CURRAGH TO RESTORE ORDER.

In the House of Commons this afternoon Captain Craig asked the Chief Secretary for Ireland whether he was prepared to make any statement in regard to the situation in Dublin.

Mr. Birrell said:—

At noon yesterday a grave disturbance broke out in Dublin. The Post Office was forcibly taken possession of, and telegraphic communication was cut off.

In the course of the day forces arrived from the Curragh, and the situation is now well in hand, although communication is exceedingly difficult.

I am not now able to give any further particulars, but the House may take it from me that the situation is now well in hand.

#### Twelve Lives Lost.

Captain Craig.—Can the right hon. gentleman state whether any arrests have been made?

Mr. Birrell.—That is a question I cannot answer—whether any arrests have been made.

Sir E. Carson.—Have any lives been lost?

Mr. Birrell.—Yes, sir.

An Hon. Member.—How many, and on which side?

Mr. Birrell.—I should say twelve, speaking from information which has reached me.

#### "In the Hands of Rebels."

Colonel Sharman Crawford.—Up to seven o'clock last night, was the Government in the hands of the rebels?

Mr. Birrell.—That is again a question I cannot definitely answer. They were in possession of four or five different parts of the city. They were not in possession of the whole place.

#### The Telegraph Wires.

Sir J. Lonsdale.—Is telegraphic communication interrupted between Ireland and England?

Mr. Birrell.—During this morning I have been in communication, but I have had great difficulty in getting through. I have had some communication by telegraph.

Captain Faber.—Have any soldiers' lives been lost?

Mr. Birrell.—I am afraid that is so—four or five.

### IRISH SITUATION.

#### PREMIER'S CONFERENCE WITH CHIEF SECRETARY.

The Prime Minister, who returned to Downing-street this morning, did not, as was expected, attend the Anzac service at Westminster Abbey.

The right hon. gentleman had consultations

with some of his colleagues, including the Chief Secretary for Ireland and the Home Secretary.

### SIR R. CASEMENT.

#### TRAITOR BROUGHT TO LONDON FOR TRIAL.

The notorious traitor Sir Roger Casement, whose vain attempts to suborn Irish prisoners in Germany have been followed by his participation in an abortive scheme to land arms in Ireland, is now in London for trial. The attempt was made by a German auxiliary cruiser disguised as a neutral ship along with a U boat between April 20 and 21. But the auxiliary was sunk and a number of prisoners made, including Casement.

This afternoon the Press Bureau issued the following statement:—

Sir Roger Casement, whose arrest in connection with the abortive attempt to land arms in Ireland from a German vessel was announced yesterday, was brought to London on Sunday morning.

He was met at Euston by officers from Scotland Yard, and is now detained in military custody.

It is understood that evidence as to his proceedings in Germany since the outbreak of war will be produced at his trial.

A sketch of Sir Roger Casement's career appears on another page.

### MR. BILLING'S QUESTION.

#### WILL THIS TRAITOR BE SHOT AT ONCE?

Mr. Pemberton Billing asked whether Sir Roger Casement had been brought to London, and whether this traitor would be shot forthwith.

Mr. Asquith said he did not think that question should be put to him.

Secret Session of Parliament: Full report of the preliminary proceedings will be found on Page 7.

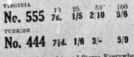

# A timely reminder

IDEA № 6
## THE TOPICAL AD

A topical ad plays off a recent event, or the time of year. The advertiser hopes that by associating themselves with something that is in the public consciousness, they will make their brand top-of-mind.

Topical ads in newspapers have been around for nearly as long as newspapers themselves. On 2 September 1686, Charles V of Lorraine led a Christian army that inflicted a major defeat on a Turkish army at Buda in Hungary ... and by 1 November, map and printseller John Oliver had placed an ad on the back page of the *London Gazette* advertising 'A curious Delineation of the Storming of Buda'.

One of the longest-running topical campaigns is the association of Coke with Christmas. Starting in 1931, magazine ads for Coca-Cola appeared at Christmastime, featuring Santa as a kind, jolly man in a red suit; he was drinking a Coke, to promote the idea that it was not just a drink for summer. Prior to Coke's campaign, there had not been any set style for the depiction of St Nick – he was sometimes tall, some-times thin and sometimes curiously elf-like. Today we all know what Santa looks like – he looks like the image created for him in Coca-Cola's advertising.

Topical ads can successfully spring-board off any specific time of the year, such as Mother's Day, New Year's Day or Valentine's Day. April Fools' Day is a popular candidate for topical humour. But they can also be based on one-off events, such as a celebrity news item, the departure of a prime minister or the result of a sporting event. One could argue that it requires disproportionate effort on the part of both marketer and agency to create an ad that will run only once. On the other hand, an ad only *has* to run once if it is good enough. Plus, it can be rather useful for big brands to run topical ads, since it makes them appear nimble and light on their feet, and not the corporate behemoths they are in reality. ■

TEARS DRY FASTER IN THE SUN

Make England's exit easier to deal with.

where are you going?

majorca, malaga, alicante
from
£50.99*
one way
inc. taxes

europe by
easyJet

# Talent imitates, genius steals

IDEA № 7

# APPROPRIATION

Just as Marcel Duchamp appropriated a urinal and proclaimed it as his own work of art, advertising has long made use of material from other sources. Some argue that there is nothing wrong with taking inspiration; others call it a rip-off.

Early advertising signwriters copied the great painters of the day, and TV ads have always borrowed styles – or entire scenes – from famous movies: in trying to position a product, it is helpful to base an ad around something already familiar to the audience, so that the values you want to communicate are understood quickly and easily.

Conversely, advertising also looks to more obscure influences, in order to bring something fresh to the general public. Henri de Toulouse-Lautrec borrowed from Japanese art to create his famous posters for the Moulin Rouge in the 1890s. And today the practice is more widespread than ever, since websites like YouTube and FFFFOUND

enable agencies to trawl the internet for interesting ideas from young artists and directors, and copy them. (It might be argued that advertising creatives ought to come up with their own ideas. But since ad agencies need hundreds of ideas a year, it is perhaps not surprising that creatives cast their nets.)

The legal status of appropriating other people's ideas is clear – it is legal. This was clarified in a court case in 1997, when director Mehdi Norowzian sued Guinness, claiming that its 1994 commercial 'Anticipation', which featured a man dancing around a pint, infringed the copyright of a short film he had created called *Joy*. Norowzian lost. Although the idea was the same,

the judgement confirmed that an idea cannot be protected by copyright, only its execution; because Guinness had created their own version of the idea, they had done nothing illegal.

The murkier question is whether appropriation is ethical. Considering that William Shakespeare took many of his plots from the Greeks, and Pablo Picasso borrowed themes from African art, it seems bizarre that lowly advertising creatives should be criticized for it. On the other hand, it seems unfair that up-and-coming young artists and film-makers have their ideas used by international ad agencies, and do not get paid. ∎

LEFT: *Honda's 2012 Super Bowl ad borrowed the plot – and lead actor – from the movie* Ferris Bueller's Day Off.

*Famous poster by Toulouse-Lautrec advertising a cabaret at the Ambassadeurs club in Paris, 1892 (right). Lautrec appropriated the style of 18th-century Japanese woodcuts depicting kabuki performers (example above).*

*A creative business*

# THE ADVERTISING AGENCY

The first advertising agencies were just bulk-buyers of ad space. The industry only took off when they began to *create* as well as place their clients' ads.

The first recorded British advertising agent was a William Taylor, who described himself as 'an Agent to County Printers' in an advertisement in the *Maidstone Journal* in 1786, and the first American ad agency was opened by Volney B. Palmer in Philadelphia, 1842. These early agencies bought large amounts of ad space in newspapers in return for a discount, then re-sold it (at a slightly smaller discount) to advertisers. The actual ad was still prepared by the advertiser; the only service the agencies offered their clients was a cheaper cost of media.

In 1800, however, James White founded an agency in London that offered to plan, create and execute advertising campaigns for its customers – it was the first 'full service' agency. The first in the US was N. W. Ayer & Son, founded in 1869. Their clients included John Wanamaker department stores, Singer sewing-machines and Pond's beauty cream. Now advertising agencies were positioning themselves as experts in the field of advertising, not just media buying. They promised their clients access to copywriters who could create ads more powerful than the client could themselves – a model that essentially still holds true today. It succeeded to the extent that by 1906 there were over 400 advertising agencies in London. In 1947, JWT became the first agency to surpass $100 million in billings, and in 1962 Papert Koenig Lois was the first to go public. Advertising had almost become respectable.

Nowadays, agencies come in all shapes and sizes, from local hot shops (see **No. 48, The Hot Shop**) to giant international holding companies like Dentsu and WPP. Some specialize in certain fields, such as retail or youth marketing, and some in certain media, such as digital agencies like R/GA and Razorfish. But, despite these differences, ad agencies all around the world are remarkably similar. They all employ staff in the same four basic functions – account management, planning, creative and production; they all pitch against each other ferociously for new accounts; and most pay far too much attention to creative awards.

Companies occasionally experiment with taking their advertising in-house – such as Italian fashion brand Benetton, which did without the services of an ad agency for an 18-year period (1982–2000), instead employing photographer Oliviero Toscani to create a controversial series of advertisements. But although ad agencies are increasingly criticized as expensive and inflexible, no better model has yet been developed, and over 95 per cent of worldwide advertising is still created through an agency. ∎

ABOVE: *Print campaign by Dentsu Malaysia. Dentsu is by far the largest agency group in Asia.*

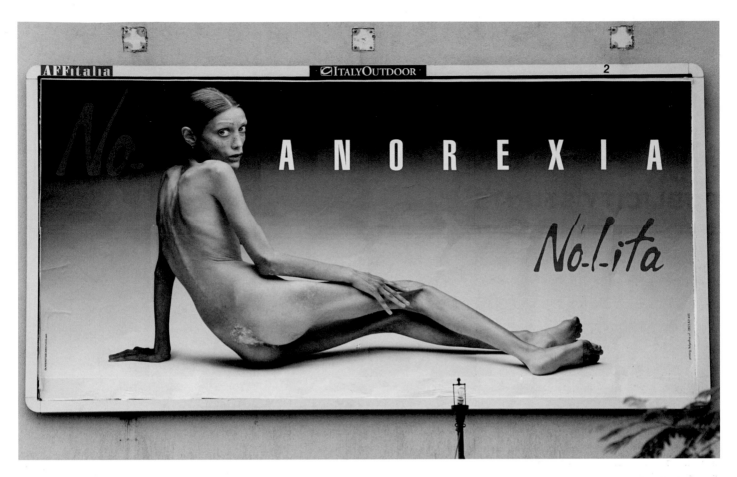

'Advertising had almost become acceptable.'

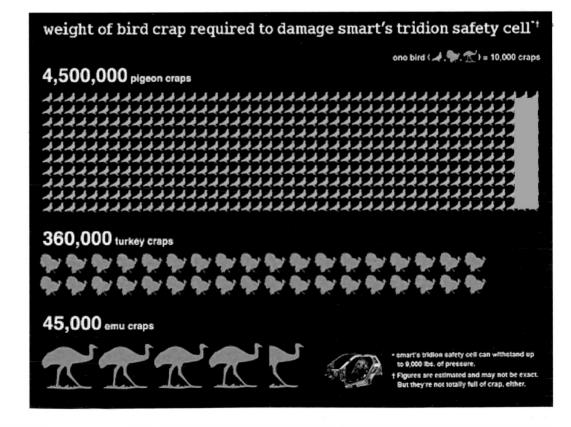

*ABOVE: Controversial 2007 poster for Italian fashion brand Nolita, created not through an ad agency but directly by the photographer, Oliviero Toscani.*

*RIGHT: Digital agency Razorfish sent this clever riposte to a Twitter user who had joked: 'Saw a bird crap on a Smart car. Totaled it.'*

# The art of hoopla

IDEA № 9

# PUBLICITY STUNTS

Rather than pay for advertising space, a publicity stunt is an attempt to garner editorial coverage in newspapers, on TV and on the internet. The stunt itself may only be seen by a few, but if it is bizarre or controversial enough, the resulting PR could be seen by millions – and it is all free advertising.

*Stunnt* was a Middle English word meaning 'foolish' or 'short-witted', and there is definitely a sense of glorious stupidity about successful stunts – as their most famous early exponent, showman P. T. Barnum, put it: 'The bigger the humbug, the better people will like it.' Publicity stunts took off in tandem with the growth of newspapers in the first decades of the nineteenth century, and in 1878 the word 'stunt' entered the dictionary as 'an unusual or difficult feat ... especially one performed chiefly to gain publicity'.

The enduring popularity of stunts is due to the media having acres of newsprint and huge chunks of live TV to fill every day, meaning that their appetite for the novel is insatiable. In addition to unusualness, most successful stunts have to be visual, since they are going to appear either on TV or as a photo in newspapers.

The perennial challenge for the PR agencies and ad agencies who create publicity stunts is to design them in such a way that the brand message is integral, and not overshadowed. It is easy enough to attract attention with an off-the-wall event such as swallowing live goldfish or dropping turkeys from a helicopter, but if the stunt does not promote the concept behind it, then it is wasted energy.

Nowadays, stunts are often filmed, and the footage released to TV or the internet. For the launch of TV channel TNT in Belgium, ad agency Duval Guillaume placed a big red button in a quiet square and labelled it 'Push to add drama'. When an unsuspecting member of the public pushed the button, a ridiculously over-dramatic live stunt unfolded, involving kung-fu ambulancemen and police exchanging gunfire with criminals, while a woman in a red bikini cruised past on a motorbike. The resulting YouTube film has scored over 48 million views. In 2011, the same agency filled a cinema with 148 tough-looking bikers, and any members of the public brave enough to take up their seats were rewarded with the brand message: 'That calls for a Carlsberg.' The stunt has been viewed 14 million times on YouTube. ∎

TOP RIGHT: *Publicity stunt promoting a TV series called* The Naked Office, *2010.*

LEFT: *Intimidating bikers in a 2011 stunt for Danish brewer Carlsberg.*

OPPOSITE: *Ecologically-conscious stunt for the launch of Eden, a natural history TV channel, in 2009.*

"The bigger the humbug, the better
people will like it.'"

ABOVE: *This huge billboard in New York City's SoHo neighbourhood prompted The American Family Association to launch an appeal that generated over 15,000 email complaints to Calvin Klein.*

OPPOSITE: *This 2007 British government anti-smoking campaign attracted 774 complaints. But it was not banned, since the shock tactics were justified by the subject matter.*

# Keeping it legal

IDEA № 10
# REGULATION

The rise of 'quack' advertisements touting miracle cures and instant beauty treatments became a serious problem in the nineteenth century, and ushered in the regulation of advertising content.

Highly dependent on advertising for their revenues, newspapers in the 1800s exerted little censorship over ads. The *Public Ledger* of Philadelphia's policy was to 'admit any advertisement of any thing ... within the boundaries of decency and morals'. But they accepted ads for patented medicines claiming to be cure-alls for health problems, and creams that supposedly removed freckles. In 1914, the Federal Trade Commission Act was passed in the US, giving the FTC powers to issue cease-and-desist orders against dishonest advertising. In the UK, the Advertising Association issued a code of ethics in 1924.

In 1964, after the US Surgeon General determined that smoking is 'hazardous to your health', many publications took it upon themselves to ban cigarette ads. Ironically, constraints on alcohol and cigarette advertising arguably led to greater creativity in

these areas – like the famous Silk Cut and Benson & Hedges campaigns. Cigarette advertising is now banned in many countries. (See also **No. 52, Principles**.)

The regulation of advertising is carried out in most countries by a mixture of government legislation and self-regulation, and varies enormously around the world. Tobacco can still legally be advertised on TV in Indonesia, whereas in Russia not only has tobacco advertising been completely banned, as of 2012 so has alcohol advertising. The most common restrictions are on advertising that is misleading, illegal, offensive or (in the case of certain product categories such as junk food) targets children. The UK regulator summarizes its remit as ensuring that advertising is 'legal, decent, honest and truthful'.

Some advertisers deliberately sail close to the wind. Their reasoning is that they may offend a minority, but cut

through with the majority. Social media plays an increasingly important role in whipping up controversies. If a member of the public spots an ad they do not like, it can be up on Twitter within seconds. Although in most developed countries TV ads are pre-cleared by the regulators, it can still be hard to predict what people will find offensive. The most complained-about British television ad of all time was for KFC, but not because of any bad language or sexual content – it featured people talking with their mouths full. ∎

NHS

The average smoker needs over five thousand cigarettes a year.

Get unhooked. Call 0800 169 0 169 or visit getunhooked.co.uk

SMOKEFREE

# Ads go glossy

The new mobile
HOTSPOT.

Place your NFC-enabled Android™ smartphone here to test-drive the Lexus Enform® App Suite† on the industry's first available 12.3-inch high-resolution split-screen multimedia display.
Or visit LexusAppSuite.com.

The All-New 2013 GS ⊕ **LEXUS**

## IDEA № 11
# THE MAGAZINE

After decades of staid, long copy-based newspaper ads, magazines began to offer advertisers a bolder, more visual way to sell their products. Magazines became a glitzy, glamorous medium that reached a new generation of aspirational consumers.

ABOVE: *Magazine ad for an electric car, 1904*

The first true general-interest magazine was *The Gentleman's Magazine*, which began in 1731, in London. Its editor adopted the word 'magazine' from the term for military stores, because they too housed a variety of material. In 1741, Benjamin Franklin produced *The General Magazine*, the first in America. Early examples looked more like books, usually with four small pages of dense print, and perhaps half a column of classified ads. At first only the upper classes read magazines (they were expensive), but in the 1880s, American magazines *McClure's* and *Munsey's* exploited falling print costs to drop their prices, and achieved huge circulations.

In the 1890s, following the invention of the halftone process, magazines were able to include photos; colour followed in the 1920s and took off in magazines such as *Time* and *Life* in the US, and *The Sunday Times Magazine* in the UK – suddenly slick photography became as important in ads as persuasive copy. Innovations including full-bleed photography and the new language of graphic design gave magazine ads unprecedented impact.

Advertisers have had a long-running love affair with magazines – perhaps not surprisingly, since a copy of a magazine is usually passed between several readers, meaning multiple people will see their ad. Plus, a magazine stays in the home for longer than a newspaper, so an ad may be viewed repeatedly. And better still, the reader may be exposed to an ad for as long as five minutes, if they are hooked by the article on the facing page. Conveniently, trade and specialty magazines enable the targeting of niche audiences, from runners to computer owners.

Today, magazine sales are on the decline, although many publications are migrating to the internet and having success online or as apps. Print magazines are also adopting new technologies, with advertising at the forefront. For example, *Wired* magazine recently teamed up with Lexus to create the first print ad embedded with a near-field communications, or NFC, tag. When the reader places an NFC-enabled phone over the ad, they experience a demo of the car's dashboard. ■

## The Wizard of Aah's...
## new 1966 Fairlane convertible!

Now Fairlane swings out with a great new look, an eager new personality, a wide new range of models—including three of the newest convertibles on the road! You get the idea when you take your first look at the '66 Fairlane GT convertible. Standard equipment includes bucket seats, sporty console, specially sporty GT identification and wheel covers, big 390 cubic-inch V-8, and more. GT has options like GT/A, which means Sportshift Cruise-O-Matic, our new automatic transmission that you can also shift like a manual. Some car! New this year too are an XL convertible, a Squire wagon with Magic Doorgate (swings open like a door for people *and* swings down like a tailgate for cargo!). This year we re-invented Fairlane. Drive one today and see!

1966 Fairlane GT Convertible

AMERICA'S
TOTAL PERFORMANCE CARS
# FORD
MUSTANG · FALCON · FAIRLANE · FORD · THUNDERBIRD

'Advertisers have had a long-running
love affair with magazines.'

*Sex sells*

IDEA № 12
# SEX IN ADVERTISING

Sexual imagery has gone from being non-existent in the early days of advertising, to virtually omnipresent today. But the question of whether it actually works is still up for debate.

Advertising's acknowledgement of sex was subdued for a long time, by influences such as religion, conservatism and the strictness of Victorian and early twentieth-century moral standards. There were occasional veiled references to 'passion' in the copy for beauty ads – such as a famous Lux soap ad from 1935, which used the slogan 'How to keep romance aflame' – but advertising was very chaste from a visual point of view.

That changed with the advent of the 'pin-up' in World War II; after observing the popularity of models such as Betty Grable and Ginger Rogers, advertisers jumped on the bandwagon. The launch of *Playboy* magazine in 1953 brought erotica to mass culture, and was enthusiastically embraced by marketers, keen to reach its affluent male audience.

Then the 1960s came, and with them a much greater tolerance for sexy advertising, since advertising reflects the attitudes of society, although in hindsight, many ads of this era are more notable for their sexism than their sexiness. Today, sex in advertising is more explicit than ever, and the male body is now fetishized almost as frequently as the female.

But does it work? The evidence is mixed. On the one hand, research shows that sexy ads achieve significantly above-average recall scores, performing equally well among both men and women. But on the other hand, they also generate a higher level of negative feelings and complaints.

Many marketers prefer to steer clear of the area, partly from an unwillingness to court controversy, and partly from a belief that while nudity certainly grabs a viewer's attention, it may not be an effective brand-builder for a product that has no relevance to sex. But they are increasingly in the minority. A recent study found that almost three-quarters of ads in magazines were offering a sex-related brand benefit, such as looking or feeling more attractive. ■

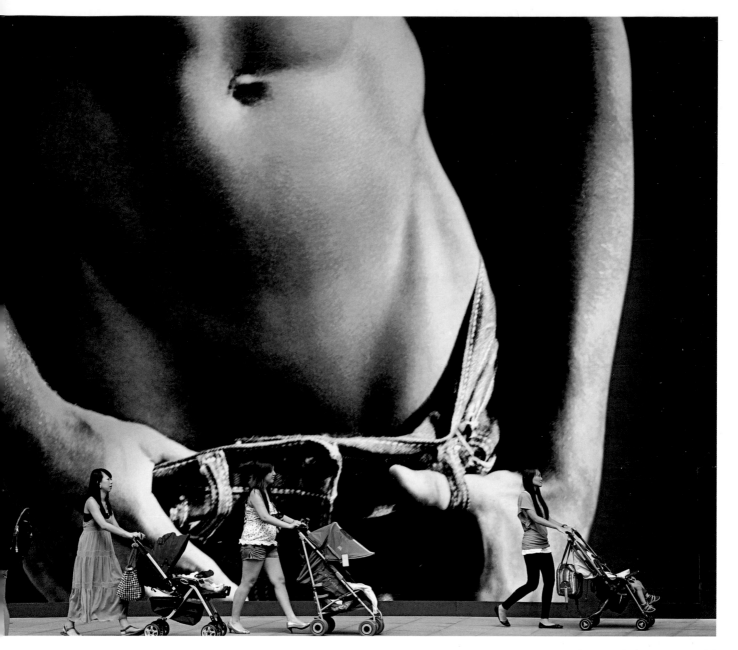

'Sexy ads achieve significantly above-average recall scores.'

*ABOVE: Men's bodies too are now being used to sell products. To the extent that in this example, an Abercrombie and Fitch billboard in Singapore, the product itself is barely visible.*

*RIGHT: US clothing retailer American Apparel has become notorious for its overtly sexual sell.*

# Sale by mail

IDEA № 13
## CATALOGUES

Print ads require a consumer to notice a product, love it and then go to a store to buy it. But catalogues combine an advertisement for a product with an order form right there – and, often, easy credit terms too – making them a powerfully direct form of selling.

As early as 1498, publisher Aldus Manutius released a catalogue of books for sale in Venice. In 1667, William Lucas created a gardening catalogue in London. One of the first American catalogues was produced by Benjamin Franklin in 1744, selling scientific and academic books. And famous entrepreneurs such as Josiah Wedgwood and Thomas Edison made mini-catalogues or pamphlets to market their wares.

But the catalogue business really took off when Aaron Montgomery Ward published his first in 1872. It was a single sheet, listing 163 items. Within two years, the catalogue grew to 8 pages, and by 1884 it contained 240 pages, with thousands of items, almost all of them illustrated with a woodcut. In 1888, a major competitor emerged with the launch of the first Sears catalogue.

The huge size of the US meant that many people lived a great distance from a large town (in fact the majority of the American population lived in the countryside until about 1920). In the catalogues, Americans could find far more products than they would ever see in their local general store. And because Sears and Montgomery Ward bought in such quantity, the prices were cheaper than they could find locally. These catalogues became so powerful they were even used to sell houses and cars.

The ability to showcase products remotely, which improved still further with the advent of photography, plus the length of time a catalogue tends to remain in the home, helped make catalogues an effective marketing tool, despite their high cost of production and distribution.

Today, the mail-order catalogue industry is worth approximately $100 billion in the US, despite the invention of the internet, which has made a company's website an alternative way to order goods for home delivery. Some catalogue merchants such as Bloomingdale's have suspended their printed catalogues and now sell only via the internet. But other catalogues are surviving by migrating to tablet computers, and aggregator websites such as Zappalog allow users to browse multiple catalogues without receiving any in the mail. A greener alternative, and financially more efficient too. ∎

# Ski-look Family Sleepwear

**1** Girls' PERMA-PREST®
Footed Pajama. Polyester
and acrylic knit. Long sleeve
pullover top is white with red
neckband and sleeves. Polyester rib-knit cuffs and neckband; screen print on front.
Red pants with elasticized
waist, non-skid vinyl soles.
To retain flame resistant
properties, machine wash,
warm using any detergent but
not soap. Use no bleach.
Tumble dry. No ironing.
Girls' sizes 7, 8, 10, 12, 14.
*State size. See Chart 1 on pg.
77. Shipping weight 13 oz.*
77 C 3833F.............$7.99

( **2 thru 5** ) Dacron® polyester
and Orlon® acrylic knit. Long
sleeve pullover tops are white
with red sleeves, screen print
design on front. Red pants
with elasticized waist. Ribbed
neckband. Rib knit cuffs at
wrist and ankles. To retain
flame resistant properties,
machine wash, warm using
any detergent but not soap.
Use no bleach. Tumble dry.

**2** **Women's.** Red neckband.
Bust sizes S(32–34); M(36)
or L(38–40). State letter size.
S, M or L.
Shipping weight 1 lb.
38 C 28101F.............$9.99
*Reg. DuPont*

**3** **Men's.** Red neckband. Fly
front. Chest sizes S(34–
36); M(38–42); XL(46–48).
State letter size S, M, L or
XL.
Shipping weight 1 lb.
33 C 13606F.............$9.99

**4** **Children's.** Red neckband. State size 2, 3, 4, 5, 6
or 6x, not age. See Chart 2 pg.
71.
Shipping weight 1 lb.
29 C 32871F.............$5.49

**5** **Boys'.** Red neckband. Fly
front. State size 8–10, or
12–14. See Chart 2 page 61.
Shipping weight 14 oz.
43 C 4525F.............$6.49

*Just call Sears
and say "Charge It"
. . see page 277*

# As seen on screen

# PRODUCT PLACEMENT

Product placement is the art of inserting products into films, TV shows and video games – often so seamlessly that the audience does not even know they are being sold to.

It may be as minimal as a logo visible in shot, but it can also go much further – a product may become an integral part of the storyline, like Tom Hanks's determination to deliver a FedEx-branded package in the movie *Castaway* (2000). The practice actually began with paid mentions for products in nineteenth-century novels. In the 1890s, Lever Brothers placed their soap products in some of the earliest movies. And it was common in the silent movie era: *Wings* (1927), winner of the first-ever Oscar for Best Picture, featured a plug for Hershey's chocolate. But product placement accelerated in the 1980s, fuelled by successes such as the placement of Ray-Ban sunglasses in the movie *Top Gun* (1986), which generated a 40 per cent increase in sales for their Aviator brand.

Reality TV has become adept at integrating products, such as the 'advertising challenges' on *The Apprentice* (which are, in reality, paid placements by the manufacturer) and the Coca-Cola cups ever-present on the *American Idol* judges' table. It also occurs in music videos, such as the Stolichnaya vodka placement in the video for Eminem's 'Love The Way You Lie' (2010), and in songs themselves, with rappers being paid to mention certain brands in their lyrics.

A new phenomenon known as digital product placement is the art of inserting products *after* a film has been shot. This has even been used to replace out-of-date products in old TV shows with current brands.

Criticism of the practice emerged as early as 1919, when a US movie-trade magazine denounced the inclusion of Red Crown Gasoline in a film called *The Garage*, starring Fatty Arbuckle. In 2012, a consumer group called Commercial Alert objected that it is 'an affront to basic honesty' since the paid-for nature of the placement is not disclosed, and the Writers Guild of America has raised objection to 'viewers being sold products without their knowledge'. Nevertheless, product placement has become an $8 billion a year industry, offering advertisers the chance to be associated with stars and TV programmes that enhance their brand image. ■

OPPOSITE TOP: *The movie* Wayne's World *(1992) employed extensive product placement, but also satirized the phenomenon.*

OPPOSITE BOTTOM: *The* American Idol *judges are always seen behind Coca-Cola cups.*

ABOVE: *Audi designed a car specifically to be featured in* I, Robot *(2004). The product placement successfully boosted the brand's scores for criteria such as attractiveness, distinctiveness and affinity.*

*Spokespeople, and spokescreatures*

IDEA № 15
# BRAND CHARACTERS

The invention of brand characters brought personality and emotion into what had previously been the rather staid and dry world of advertising.

Brand characters evolved out of trademarks. One of the earliest was the Quaker Oats man – in 1877 Quaker Mills trademarked 'a man in Quaker garb' to identify their brand of oats; they then began to use an illustration of a Quaker man on their pack, and in their advertising. A wide variety of characters have been successfully deployed by brands, from humans (Ronald McDonald, Captain Birdseye) to animals (the GEICO Gecko, Tony the Tiger) and even inanimate objects brought to life (the Michelin Man, the M&Ms).

Their primary purpose is to infuse brands with the desired personality – the Quaker man was chosen because the cereal's makers wanted to transcribe the Quaker values of integrity, honesty and purity to their product. They also help personify companies that sell non-visual products, such as insurance (Aleksandr the Meerkat for CompareTheMarket. com, the Aflac duck), or dull ones such as toilet paper (Mr Whipple, the Charmin bears). In short, brand characters – even the mascots which are actually animals – are there to give brands a human touch.

Perhaps because animals put us at ease, and we find them likeable and humorous, animal characters are a popular choice. However, it is not essential for a mascot to be cuddly. Burger King's 'The King' character was considered creepy by many, but was by and large popular with his target audience of young men.

Occasionally, brand characters fail if they become more famous than the brand itself, or if the product has a distinctive feature or benefit and the character detracts from it. But in highly competitive categories where there is little to differentiate the players, they can be a powerful marketing tool. The Aflac duck, for example, debuted in 2000 and in the first year after his introduction, sales went up 29 per cent. After two years, name recognition had increased by 67 per cent. Today the duck has 165,000 Facebook fans. ■

ABOVE: *The original Quaker Oats man (1877). The character has been updated just three times since its creation.*

LEFT: *Would a company called the Government Employees Insurance Company have become so popular with the American public if their ad agency had not realized that the word GEICO sounded a little like 'gecko'?*

OPPOSITE: *Less than a month after the introduction of the cowboy in its print advertising, Marlboro became the number one brand in Greater New York. It was soon the best-selling cigarette brand in the world.*

# Catchy encapsulations

## IDEA Nº 16
# SLOGANS

*Liberté, égalité, fraternité* was the slogan of the French Revolution more than 200 years ago but it still has resonance today. And that is exactly what the best brand slogans aspire to – memorability and persuasive power.

In the UK, they are known as endlines or straplines; in the US they are called taglines or tags. The earliest advertising slogan was for Ivory soap, which was introduced in 1879 with a pledge that it was '99 and $^{44}/_{100}$% pure'. This proved so effective that the company began to use it as a sign-off to all their advertisements.

As the Industrial Revolution gathered pace and more and more branded products were introduced, slogans helped a brand stand out in an increasingly competitive marketplace, quickly telling consumers what the product stood for, in an appealing manner. Some evolved out of headlines, such as automobile brand Packard's 'Ask the man who owns one' (1901), but soon they came to be custom-written, and by the 1920s no ad was complete without one.

For impact and memorability, taglines frequently use rhetorical devices such as repetition ('Be all that you can be'),

reversal ('Our food is fresh. Our customers are spoiled'), rhyme (wartime slogan 'Loose lips sink ships') and alliteration (Brylcreem's 'A little dab'll do ya'). The use of catchy, rhyming endlines had its heyday in the 1970s and 80s, with examples such as 'Hello Tosh, gotta Toshiba?' and 'You can break a brolly but you can't knacker a Knirps' (for Knirps umbrellas). Today, taglines are becoming ever shorter, sometimes reducing to a single word – like 'Passion' or 'Joy' – which unfortunately can make them banal.

It is a widespread misconception that a slogan has to be short to be catchy: in fact, a few extra words are often required to create a striking rhyme or rhythm – for example, it would have been quicker for FedEx to adopt the one-word tagline 'Overnight', but opting for the longer 'When it absolutely, positively has to be there overnight' gave the tag its memorable turn of phrase. The line also captured the emotional state of the

package-sender – a desire for certainty. An emotional payload is what elevates the best taglines beyond being mere clever wordplay. After all, advertising is seduction ... and without emotion, seduction cannot take place. ∎

OPPOSITE BOTTOM: *Early tagline for Packard motor cars, 1901*

ABOVE: *McDonald's 'i'm lovin' it' slogan, used widely around the world since 2003, was in fact created by a German ad agency – Heye & Partner – as 'ich liebe es'.*

RIGHT: *Nike's famous slogan, coined in 1988, was supposedly inspired by US murderer Gary Gilmore's last words before his execution.*

실수하지
않을 수 있을까?

JUST DO IT

*The 'torture test'*

# PRODUCT DEMONSTRATION ADS

No selling-method is more successful than someone showing you exactly how a product works, which is why the door-to-door vacuum-cleaner salesmen were so desperate to be let inside. With the arrival of TV, manufacturers realized they could beam demonstrations into every home.

Demonstration is an ancient sales technique; medieval pedlars would have demonstrated their wares in the town square. Even today, certain products continue to be sold via demonstration in street markets and department stores – particularly novelty cooking utensils that have an impressive visual effect.

The demonstration has been a popular advertising approach since advertising first began; early newspaper ads frequently showed the 'wondrous results' of miracle cures and cosmetics. In the 1920s, the demonstration ad increased in sophistication – agencies began to dramatize their demonstrations, putting the product through its paces in exaggerated scenarios, for instance an elephant standing on a suitcase to show how tough it is. This type of ad is known as a 'torture test'.

The demonstration style became especially popular with the advent of television, a medium ideal for demonstrating how something works since it can show a visual narrative unfolding. The soap-powder manufacturers enthusiastically adopted the genre, and vied to show viewers how white their washing powders washed. By the 1980s, however, over-use had made the demo ad seem hackneyed, and suspicion of 'special-effects trickery' had compromized its credibility.

Demonstration ads are occasionally still seen today, but normally only when a product genuinely does something new and amazing – in which case it would perhaps be wrong for advertising flimflam to get in the way. Apple, for example, often runs very simple product demo ads: the launch ads in 2007 for the iPhone simply showed a finger flicking the touch-screen.

The demonstration is also sometimes used as an ironic construct. For example, an award-winning ad for long-lasting batteries showed a man taking multiple pictures with a digital camera, and when the flash stopped working, he took the batteries out – and threw the camera away. The audience knows that this demonstration is not intended to be taken at face value, but the verve of the battery-maker impresses nonetheless. ∎

ABOVE: *The dramatized demonstration. Poster for Araldite adhesive, 1983.*

OPPOSITE TOP: *'Will it Blend?' is the title of a successful series of viral marketing videos for Blendtec blenders. The campaign is pure product demonstration.*

OPPOSITE BOTTOM: *Still from a 2012 TV ad demonstrating the Smart car's 'Tridion' safety cell.*

Tridion safety cell mounted on stationary base. Do not attempt

# Snipping out savings

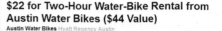

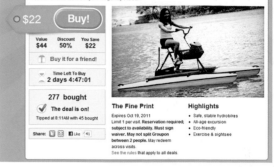

IDEA № 18
# COUPONS

An incredible *3 billion* coupons a year are redeemed in the United States. The secret of their success? It is not just financial savings they provide, but pleasure – a survey showed that 96 per cent of Americans would continue to clip coupons even if they won the lottery.

The very first coupons were issued in 1887, by Coca-Cola, to give away a free Coke. The tactic was so successful that by 1913, one in nine Americans had received a free Coca-Cola. Coupon use grew dramatically during the depression years of the 1930s, and by 1965 half of all American families were cutting coupons. Today, more than 2,800 different companies offer coupons in the US, and consumers are redeeming them for a total annual saving of $4.6 billion.

Coupons are more than just a technique for increasing sales (albeit at a slightly reduced margin) – they prevent a sale going to a competitor, and bring customers into the store where they may make further purchases on impulse. They are also used as a research method. By sending out coupons for different amounts to different areas, or to different demographic groups, companies can measure the price sensitivity of different buyers, and adjust their pricing policies accordingly.

A store issuing vouchers for what seems like an unbelievable 30 or 40 per cent discount is in fact doing nothing different to holding a sale, but with the added benefit that it avoids the brand-cheapening effect of having 'SALE!' signs in their windows.

Newspapers are still the most popular means to distribute coupons, but online and mobile couponing is on the rise (see **No.80, Mobile**). Although online coupons account for only 1 per cent of all coupons distributed, they account for 10 per cent of all redemptions. Part of the explanation is that printable discount vouchers have become a viral marketing phenomenon.

The latest twist for the discount voucher has seen it 'go social' in the form of group buying sites, which have mushroomed in recent years. The largest of these sites, Groupon, has over 42 million active customers. ∎

☐ **Yes,** let's cancel Third World debt and give the world's poorest countries a glimmer of hope.

Please send this coupon to Jubilee 2000 Coalition, PO Box 10, London Sw9, Part 1 if you'd like to give further help, please enclose a cheque made payable to Jubilee 2000 Coalition or freefone 0800 1234 for credit card donations.

## JUBILEE 2000 COALITION

A debt-free start for a billion people.

☐ **No,** let's make the lazy Ethiopian spongers pay back the £7 billion they owe us.

## THE WORLD POWERS

It's our money and we want it back.

'Today more than 2,800 different companies offer coupons in the

DISTRIBUTED THROUGH
WORLD FILM
CORPORATION

From Group by MARTIN

THIRD
UNITED STATES OFFICIAL WAR PICTURE

# UNDER
# FOUR FLAGS

PRESENTED BY DIVISION OF FILMS
COMMITTEE ON PUBLIC INFORMATION
GEORGE CREEL, CHAIRMAN.

TAKEN BY THE OFFICIAL PHOTOGRAPHERS
THE ALLIED ARMIES

OFFICIAL SEAL OF
THE PEOPLES FILMS

# Commercials with popcorn

IDEA № 19
# CINEMA ADVERTISING

The arrival of cinema offered two incredible new thrills: the realism of motion, and the unreal, dream-like quality that movies can possess. Advertisers came on board almost straight away.

The first cinema in the United States – Vitascope Hall, in New Orleans – opened in 1896, and the Lumière brothers gave a demonstration of their cinematograph in London's Regent Street in the same year. Cinema advertising began soon after, in the form of simple announcements etched on to slides and projected on to the screen.

Filmed commercials were being produced as early as 1897; the very first known cinema ad featured several men in kilts, dancing merrily in front of a banner advertising Dewar's Scotch whisky. It was pure spectacle and emotion – a world away from the hard-selling copy full of reasoned argument that was the standard in print advertising. From the beginning, advertisers understood that cinema was a more visceral and less rational medium than print, and that it was especially good at creating atmosphere.

The war years saw audiences boom, and cinema advertising quickly became a major part of government propaganda campaigns. But the medium faced stiff competition with the introduction of television, and fell into a long decline that only began to reverse with the innovation of the multiplex in the 1980s. Cinema advertising has recently begun to grow again, as the cost of TV has risen, but it still represents only around 1 per cent of total adspend. As digital projection begins to replace the traditional reel-to-reel systems, which lowers production costs, that share may increase. In an increasingly distracted age, cinema benefits from offering advertisers an audience that is actually watching the screen, rather than talking to someone else in the room or playing on their iPad.

And whereas much advertising is deemed irritating by consumers, cinema advertising arguably makes a positive contribution to the overall cinema experience – surveys report that audiences actually enjoy watching cinema ads, perhaps because the marketers tend to put their most epic and youth-focused work into cinemas. Advertisers who have exploited the potential of cinema to its fullest with glamorous, escapist commercials include Mercedes, Bacardi and Dunlop tyres. ■

*ABOVE: Directed by Michael Mann and starring Benicio Del Toro, this slick 2002 cinema ad for Mercedes innovated by screening during the movie trailer sequence not the ads. It trailed an imaginary thriller called Lucky Star.*

*OPPOSITE: Wartime US government propaganda film, 1918.*

*LEFT: Some of the most successful cinema commercials are those specifically created for the medium, such as the 'Orange Film Board' campaign for mobile phone network Orange. It ran for seven years and through 24 executions, deploying numerous movie celebrities including Spike Lee.*

*Advertising behemoths*

IDEA № 20
# GLOBAL AGENCY NETWORKS

Advertising agencies have grown from smallish local businesses to become national, international and now global enterprises, the largest of which – WPP – has over 158,000 employees, and more than £10 billion in annual revenues.

J. Walter Thompson was the first agency to create an international network. The US-based agency opened its London office in 1899, and by 1930 it had established offices in some 30 countries, driven by the rapid international expansion of its clients, principally General Motors. It was followed by other American agencies such as McCann Erickson, which by 1969 was earning half its revenues through offices outside the US. Today, there are several agency networks with offices in upwards of 80 countries. These include Grey, J. Walter Thompson (JWT), Leo Burnett, McCann Erickson, Saatchi & Saatchi, Lowe + Partners, Publicis, Y&R, DDB, Ogilvy, TBWA and BBDO.

The globalization of advertising has parallelled the internationalization of business in general, and brought some of the same fears about potential global blandness and homogeneity – which have proved largely groundless, since a business as complex as an advertising agency could never be as standardized as a branch of Starbucks or McDonald's. If anything, being part of a global network has opened agencies up to cross-cultural pollination; it is now common for advertising executives to spend time in several different network offices around the world.

In the 1980s, a wave of mergers and acquisitions began, which saw the networks themselves end up in the hands of four giant holding companies – Interpublic (which owns Lowe and McCann Erickson), Omnicom (BBDO, DDB and TBWA), Publicis (Publicis, Leo Burnett, Saatchi & Saatchi) and WPP (Grey, JWT, Ogilvy, Y&R). The revenue of these 'big four' today stands at over $40 billion – nearly double the rest of the top 50.

The holding company model was met with suspicion in some quarters, but has proved a hit with investors. The entry of WPP into the FTSE 100, for example, meant that many investment funds automatically acquired its shares. Plus, WPP's scale has enabled it to negotiate contracts at a global level with international companies such as Vodafone, securing their advertising contract for every country in the world. ∎

LEFT: *The extent of the WPP holding company is fairly staggering, through a network of over 350 companies it has a presence in 110 countries and employs 170,000 people in 3,000 offices.*

*Maurice Lévy, president, Publicis Groupe (Publicis, Leo Burnett, Saatchi & Saatchi).*

*Michael Roth, chairman and CEO, Interpublic (Lowe, McCann Erickson).*

*John Wren, CEO, Omnicom (BBDO, DDB, TBWA).*

*Martin Sorrell, CEO, WPP (Grey, JWT, Ogilvy, Y&R).*

'An ad agency could never be as standardized as a branch of Starbucks or McDonald's.'

# The adsmiths

ABOVE: *TV ad for cream cakes, written by Salman Rushdie.*

OPPOSITE: *The iconic British Airways 'World's Favourite Airline' tagline was created by Geoffrey Seymour, once the UK's highest-paid copywriter.*

IDEA № 21
## CREATIVES

Originally, advertising agencies merely placed the ads, which were written by the products' manufacturers. So the first creatives did not work in ad agencies, but for household-goods and pharmaceutical companies.

The most famous was a chap called John Powers, who once claimed that 'fine writing is offensive' – he concentrated on facts. By the late 1890s, Powers was earning more than $100 a day. Gradually, ad agencies started to become 'full service' – that is, they both created and placed ads – and they hired copywriters themselves. The realization that a superior advertisement could create a disproportionate increase in a company's sales began to place a premium on the salaries of the few creatives who were consistently able to create them. The first superstar creative was probably Claude Hopkins, who in 1907 was hired by Lord & Thomas advertising at a salary of $185,000 a year. Lord & Thomas was the first agency to really take creativity seriously. Whereas most ad agencies made do with just a couple of copywriters, Lord & Thomas had a department of ten.

Later copywriting superstars included Raymond Rubicam, Rosser Reeves and David Ogilvy. The best-known UK example was Geoff Seymour, who in 1982 was poached by Charles Saatchi from CDP for the then unheard-of salary of £100,000 a year – about six times the average wage of a copywriter – and the term 'a Seymour' became adland slang for the sum of £100,000. But Seymour was worth it, creating a slew of famous campaigns such as the 'Boy on a Bike' ad for Hovis, the Paul Hogan 'It's Australian for lager' campaign for Foster's, 'Reassuringly expensive' for Stella Artois and 'The world's favourite airline' for British Airways.

Quite a number of authors made their start as advertising creatives. Salman Rushdie, for example, came up with the line 'Naughty. But nice' for cream cakes while he was at Ogilvy & Mather. Crime writer Dorothy L. Sayers created 'Just think what Toucan do' for Guinness. Joseph Heller (*Catch-22*) and Peter Carey (*Oscar and Lucinda*) both served time in creative departments too (see also **No. 67, Advertising as Fiction**). Other copywriters and art directors have gone on to be film directors, including Alan Parker (*Midnight Express*, *Mississippi Burning*), John Hughes (*The Breakfast Club*; *Planes, Trains and Automobiles*) and Tony Kaye (*American History X*). ■

LEFT: *Joseph Heller, who began* Catch-22 *in 1953 while working as a copywriter for a small New York advertising agency.*

BRITISH AIRWAYS
The world's favourite airline.

ABOVE: *The 2010 instalment of the cola wars. A Pepsi delivery driver takes a photo of a Coke delivery driver enjoying a Pepsi Max; commercial by TBWA\Chiat\Day.*

LEFT: *A 2012 commercial for SodaStream took on the whole soft drinks category, showing soda bottles dissolving each time a person made a drink using a SodaStream machine.*

OPPOSITE: *For years, Apple ran ads mocking Microsoft. In 2013, Samsung launched a campaign mocking Apple.*

# Knocking copy

IDEA № 22

# COMPARATIVE ADS

Despite some legal limitations on its use, which vary by country, comparative advertising has an undeniable power and is frequently used by the 'underdog' competitor – such as Pepsi vs Coke, or Mac vs PC.

The earliest case dates back to 1910 in the United States, when the makers of Hunyadi János, a brand of mineral water, sued a competitor whose ads compared their own water to Hunyadi – and lost. The ruling was that as long as a comparison was not deceptive, it was allowable. For the first time, advertisers were allowed to do more than just say 'we are the best', they could say *who* they were better than, and why.

Nevertheless, marketers for the most part avoided the strategy, believing that comparative advertising was viewed negatively by consumers, and that this negativity would rebound on to the advertiser making the comparison – a belief that is still widespread today. It was also felt that a potential descent into slanging matches could damage the credibility of advertising itself, hence comparative ads were banned on US television until 1972, when the Federal Trade Commission (FTC) issued a statement explicitly supporting comparative advertising, providing the comparisons were 'clearly identified, truthful, and non-deceptive'.

In the 1980s, during the so-called cola wars, Pepsi ran hundreds of ads in which people chose Pepsi over Coke, either when they were blindfolded or caught on hidden camera. Because of its inherent 'knocking' tone, comparative advertising is almost never employed by the market leader, but by the competitor snapping at their heels.

In the UK, using a competitor's name in comparative advertising was finally permitted only as recently as 1994, as long as the comparisons are 'fair and accurate'. Comparisons that are 'offensive' are banned, but the courts have proved lenient on this. A 2005 print ad for Ryanair, referring to the much higher costs of flying with British Airways, used the headline 'Expensive BA****DS!' BA sued, but lost. ■

# Self-promotion

RIGHT: *Several agencies have written their own slogans. McCann Erickson's, created in 1912 and still in use today, is perhaps the best known.*

IDEA Nº 23
## THE AGENCY AS BRAND

Very early in their history, agencies realized that in a competitive marketplace it was not enough to build their clients' brands – they had to build their own.

Of course, since agencies put large volumes of work into the public arena, it is largely their work that defines them: some become known for being great at populist advertising, some for cutting-edge work, some for comedy. But an agency's brand is also a function of the training given to staff, its building and decor, its dress code, even its stationery – all elements to which agencies therefore pay considerable attention.

The major benefit of having a highly regarded brand is that it helps agencies on to pitch lists, since it is said that clients only know the names of three agencies – their current one, their last one and maybe one other that people are talking about. Having a strong reputation also helps to retain existing business, and to attract talent.

Perhaps surprisingly for an industry that fervently advises clients to create distinctive personalities for their brands, some agencies fail to follow their own advice, believing that their work will speak for itself. But others, aware of the crucial importance of their agency's creative reputation, invest a significant amount of time into *pro bono* and self-initiated projects, such as Dutch agency KesselsKramer's work for the Hans Brinker Hotel, and Mother London's quirky series of football-related projects. Canadian agency John St. have defined themselves as funny and creative with self-promotional films that lampoon trends such as case-study films and cat videos.

In 2007, Minneapolis-based agency Campbell Mithun shocked the industry when it appointed another ad agency to help define its brand. CEO Jack Rooney was quoted in *Ad Age* as saying that an agency rebrand is 'a bit like heart surgery. You can't operate on yourself.' Some, however, questioned whether an agency that does not feel it can create a powerful brand for itself, would be able to do so for its clients. ∎

LEFT: *Mother London regularly produces self-promotional items, including this sticker album commemorating the England football team's failure to qualify for the 2008 European Championships. Instead of depicting players in action, the stickers showed them shopping, or watching TV.*

OPPOSITE: *The Tap Project was created by ad agency Droga5 in 2007 – it asks restaurant diners to donate $1 to Unicef each time they order tap water. Not only had the project raised almost $1 million by 2014 to support Unicef water programmes, it has also helped build the creative brand of Droga5.*

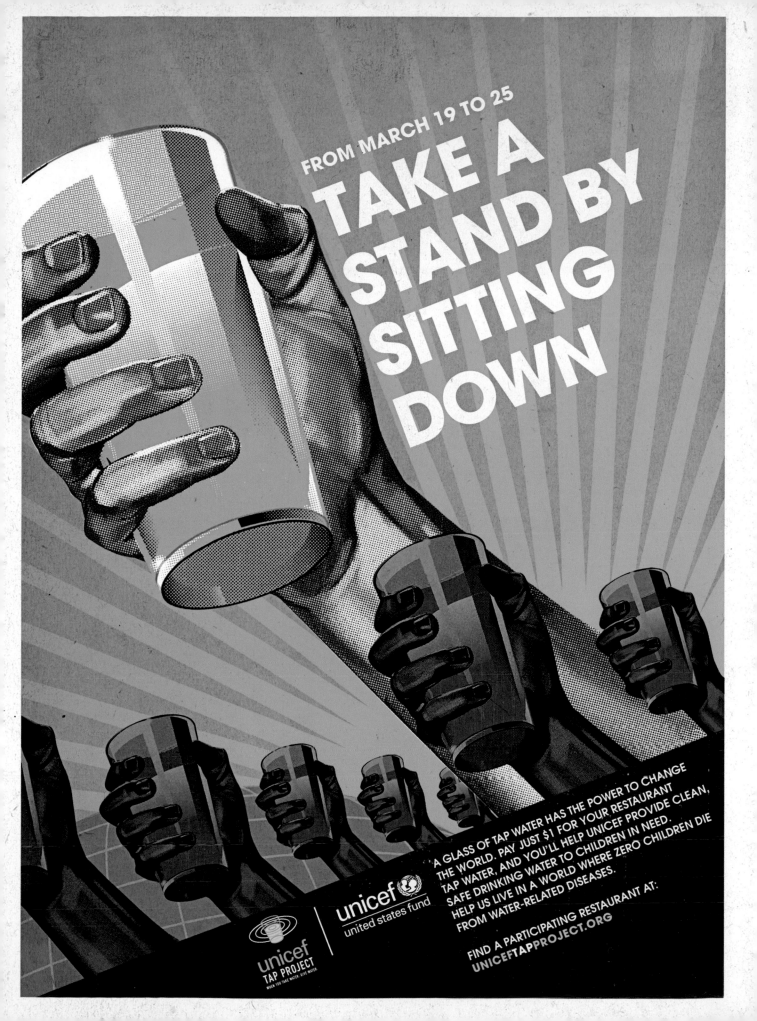

IDEA № 24

# CELEBRITY ENDORSEMENT

It began as long ago as the Victorian era, and in today's celebrity-obsessed culture has grown to the point where one in four ads on TV now uses celebrities – up from one in eight in 1996 – with advertisers spending $50 billion a year on celebrity endorsement deals.

The appeal is that the advertiser borrows from the celebrity's brand equity, receiving an instant fame boost and giving the public a clear idea of what values they stand for, via reference to the known quantity that is the celebrity. And it seems to work: one study of Facebook display ads found that ads that featured a celebrity performed 50 per cent better than those that did not.

Celebrity endorsements tend to be most effective in image-driven categories such as fashion, perfume and alcohol. They also work when a celebrity is used relevantly (e.g. an athlete endorsing Nike or Adidas), although sometimes a lateral choice can cut through, like Betty White appearing in ads for Snickers. But it can be an expensive business – Catherine Zeta-Jones was paid $20 million to endorse T-Mobile, and Nicole Kidman earned $12 million to appear in ads for Chanel No. 5.

Of course, a celebrity endorsement hits trouble if the celebrity does. Kobe Bryant was dropped by McDonald's and Nutella after he was accused of rape, Pepsi shied away from Madonna after the release of her controversial 'Like a Prayer' video, and Wrigley and the 'Got Milk?' campaign dumped Chris Brown after he pleaded guilty to assaulting Rihanna. But some brands are more forgiving. Most of Kate Moss's endorsers dropped the model after pictures were published of her snorting cocaine, but new brands stepped in to replace them, and Nike famously stood by Tiger Woods.

The newest frontier for celebrity endorsement is Twitter. Khloe Kardashian was paid $8,000 to tweet 'Want to know how Old Navy makes your butt look scary good?' and Lindsay Lohan received $3,500 for tweeting about a website called CampusLIVE. 'These challenges for college kids on #CampusLIVE are SO addicting!' tweeted Lohan, earning $53 per character, and apparently generating 2,500 visits to the website. ∎

LEFT: *Former England footballer Gary Lineker has had a long and successful association with Walkers crisps, playing a comical arch-villain in their ads since 1995.*

'Ads that featured a celebrity performed 50 per cent better than those that did not.'

# Advertising for good

"I'd rather go naked than wear fur."
– Christy Turlington

PEOPLE FOR THE ETHICAL TREATMENT OF ANIMALS PETA

IDEA Nº 25
## PUBLIC SERVICE ADVERTISING

The same techniques that sell baked beans and basketball shoes can be used to raise awareness of issues such as AIDS, animal abuse or climate change. And perhaps because of these topics' inherent drama, some of the ad industry's most creative and effective work has been in the public service.

Public service advertising (PSA) began during the American Civil War, when the government placed newspaper ads urging people to buy war bonds. The enormous success of this campaign is said to have been what persuaded manufacturers of the benefits of national advertising, and thus kick-started the modern ad industry.

The first non-governmental public service advertising was a US campaign that appeared in the early 1900s, highlighting the problem of child labour, which was co-funded by newspaper owners. With the outbreak of World War I, governments all over the world began recruitment and propaganda campaigns. The effort stepped up still further in World War II, which gave rise to famous

images such as 'Rosie the Riveter', who helped persuade 6 million American women to take up jobs in factories, replacing the men who had gone to war. 'Loose lips sink ships' and 'Careless talk costs lives' were campaigns on the theme of keeping quiet about information that might be useful to the enemy.

After the war, government efforts moved to focus on anti-litter ('Keep America/Britain Beautiful'), and then health issues, where public service advertising has had significant successes in changing behaviour, including reducing smoking rates, drink driving and speeding. Deaths in the US due to accidents where alcohol was a factor, for example, have halved in the last 40 years, though PSAs have so far been less

successful in reducing illegal drug use.

In addition to government-funded campaigns, innumerable charities and not-for-profits have harnessed the power of advertising to publicize their causes, including Amnesty International, the World Wildlife Fund and PETA. The rise of social media has enabled these organizations to publicize their cause without having to buy expensive advertising space – Greenpeace used fake Twitter accounts to undermine Shell, and made viral videos targeting Nestlé over its use of palm oil from rainforests. The *Kony* 2012 film, highlighting the brutality of African cult leader Joseph Kony's Lord's Resistance Army, spread via Facebook and reached over 90 million people. ∎

I miss my lung, Bob.

California Department Of Health Services.
Funded By The Tobacco Tax Initiative.

*OPPOSITE: Perhaps the most famous public service advertisement of all time, the 'Uncle Sam' poster, 1917.*

*TOP RIGHT: Iconic campaign by animal activist group PETA.*

*LEFT: Originated in California in 1998, these anti-smoking billboards brilliantly parodied the Marlboro ads.*

# To mailbox and inbox

IDEA № 26
# DIRECT MAIL

Americans receive over *90 billion* pieces of direct mail per year. Though sometimes derided as 'junk mail', the sending of circulars, catalogues and 'pre-approved' credit-card applications is the largest sector of the $153.3 billion direct-marketing industry.

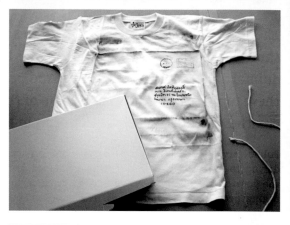

Although messages were imprinted on clay bricks and sent direct to prospects in Babylonian days, the industry properly began after nineteenth-century improvements in printing and the postal services. A direct-marketing association was then established in the US in 1917, and bulk-mail postage rates negotiated in 1928. The business grew strongly in the 1980s and 1990s due to advances in database technology – in the UK, spend more than tripled in the decade to 2003. SMS campaigns can be an effective direct marketing option, since over 90 per cent of text messages sent are opened within 15 minutes. And recently, the industry has developed a powerful (and cheap) new tool in the form of emailed marketing messages, known as electronic direct mail (EDM).

The obvious advantage that the innovation of direct mail introduced is that of targeting. For example, a nappy (diaper) manufacturer can send a mailing only to new mums – much more efficient than a poster seen by everyone from schoolkids to the elderly. Another attractive feature is its measurability. If a marketer sends out 1,000 letters and gets 100 responses they can measure their 'response rate' at 10 per cent, the kind of clearly quantifiable metric that TV and print advertising cannot provide. It also offers control – an EDM can be refined by sending different versions to different subgroups, to see exactly what works best.

The challenge the industry faces is to target the good prospects without irritating everybody else: the term 'junk mail' can be traced back to 1954, and 'spam' to 1993. In many countries, consumers can now opt out of receiving direct mail. There is also the issue of environmental impact. In the US, the Environmental Protection Agency estimates that 44 per cent of direct mail is discarded without being opened, equalling 4 million tons of waste paper a year. Several non-profit organizations, such as 41pounds.org, aim to reduce the amount of unsolicited mail that US households receive, which is estimated at ... 41 pounds per year. ∎

ABOVE: *This direct-mail piece from 2009 by Lowe Bangkok made use of the ultimate torture test for a washing-liquid sample – the postal system.*

ABOVE: *This innovative idea for Cheerios enabled Canadians to send a 'Cheer' postcard to athletes at the 2010 Winter Olympics.*

BELOW: *Award-winning direct-mail piece from 2002. Agency Archibald Ingall Stretton mailed prospects a Skoda budge, alluding to the fact that although Skoda had radically improved their cars, many people still did not feel comfortable with the marque.*

# *Libraries filled with images*

IDEA Nº 27
## STOCK SHOTS

*ABOVE: One of the most popular images sold by stock library Shutterstock.*

*BOTTOM LEFT: Some extremely well-known advertising has used stock imagery, including Apple's 'Think different' campaign, which debuted in 1997.*

The rise of 'image libraries' has enabled advertisers to create campaigns much more quickly and cheaply than by commissioning bespoke photography. These companies have now begun to offer stock footage too, which features in a surprisingly large number of TV ads.

One of the first stock photography agencies was founded in 1920 by H. Armstrong Roberts and continues today, under the name Robertstock. For many years, the agencies sold largely out-takes ('seconds') from magazine assignments. But by the 1980s, increasing demand saw stock photography become a discipline in its own right, with photographers shooting material specifically to sell to a stock library.

In the 1990s, after a period of consolidation, Getty Images and Corbis emerged as by far the two largest companies in the field. Corbis, owned by Microsoft founder Bill Gates, has a library of more than 100 million images and 500,000 video clips. Getty has an archive of 80 million still images and more than 50,000 hours of film footage, having acquired competitors such as Photodisc, Tony Stone, Hulton Getty and Jupiterimages. In recent years, mass-market availability of high-resolution digital cameras, and the ability to upload and share images via the internet, have given rise to a new breed of stock libraries selling the work of amateur photographers online, for as little as $1 per image.

Stock photography is a popular choice for ads requiring generic imagery such as landscapes, cityscapes, animals and weather. But creatives in the leading advertising agencies prefer *not* to use stock photography, believing it will be an imperfect substitute for a bespoke photoshoot, since by definition a stock image was not created to their specific idea. And marketers tend to avoid stock imagery for major projects because, since anyone can buy the shot, they run the risk of another company using the same one.

All too often, stock photography can be clichéd, such as the notorious high-fiving businessmen, and women smiling just before they bite into a pizza. However, stock photography has the undeniable advantages of speed (the image can be downloaded instantly, versus the weeks it might take to organize a shoot), cost (stock will inevitably be cheaper) and certainty (you know exactly what you are going to get, whereas with a shoot, there is always the chance it could go wrong). ∎

*Two ads for different companies (above and right), that both make use of the same stock shot by Getty Images (below).*

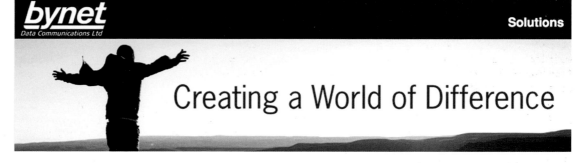

# Mad Women

RIGHT: *Woodbury's soap ad, by Helen Resor, 1915.*

BOTTOM LEFT: *Still from Lynx 'Ideal Woman' commercial, by BBH London, 2000. Creative director, Rosie Arnold.*

IDEA № 28

# WOMEN IN THE WORKPLACE

At the beginning of the twentieth century, careers were still largely for men only. But with women responsible for the majority of household purchasing, agencies began to recognize the value of their insight during the creative process, and advertising became one of the first industries to promote women to senior roles.

Mathilde C. Weil opened the M. C. Weil Agency in 1880, but the first woman to make a major impact in the advertising industry was Helen Resor, who joined J. Walter Thompson as a copywriter in 1908. Her campaign for Woodbury's soap increased sales by 1,000 per cent in eight years. Its tagline 'A skin you love to touch' showed a flair for advertising that resonated with women. Like most agencies, J. Walter Thompson had numerous brands that were specifically aimed at women – and Resor set up an all-female team of copywriters to work on them.

The first woman to become the head of a major agency was Mary Wells, a copywriter whose famous campaigns included 'Plop plop, fizz, fizz' for Alka-Seltzer, 'I love New York' and 'Quality is job one' for Ford. She also convinced Braniff Airways to splash its planes with bright colours, and dress the flight attendants in zingy designs. In 1967 she opened her own agency, Wells Rich Greene, which produced many memorable campaigns including 'Friends don't let friends drive drunk'.

Despite these outstanding examples of what they could achieve, women did suffer tremendous discrimination in advertising just as they did in every profession, but today it is quite common for agencies to employ a *majority* of women, not just working on the traditional 'female' categories such as beauty, haircare and fashion, but across every product type, and in every department, though it is fair to say they are still underrepresented in creative departments.

Prominent women in advertising today include Ogilvy Chairman Shelly Lazarus, Group Chairman and Chief Executive of AMV BBDO Cilla Snowball, Jureeporn 'Judee' Thaidumrong – one of Asia's most awarded creative talents – and BBH London Deputy Executive Creative Director and former Chair of D&AD, Rosie Arnold. ∎

*Cannes Gold-winning commercial for Smooth E, by Jureeporn 'Judee' Thaidumrong.*

'The tagline "A skin you love to touch" showed a flair for advertising that resonated with women.'

# Ads on air

IDEA № 29
## RADIO

In 1921, a group of investors declined to put money into radio, famously predicting that 'The wireless music box has no imaginable commercial value. Who would pay for a message sent to no one in particular?' Today, 95 per cent of the world's population listens to the radio.

In 1922, the first radio advertising was broadcast by WEAF in New York – it was a ten-minute talk on behalf of a real-estate firm, for which the station charged $50. In 1923, *The Eveready Hour* became the first regular radio series to be sponsored, a format that remained popular until radio-station owners realized they could make more money by selling small time-slots throughout their broadcasts, and the '30-second spot' was born. By 1938, radio had surpassed magazines in terms of adspend.

Radio advertising started much later in Europe and Canada, which had adopted a public service broadcasting model, and by the time it was officially introduced, the medium had been somewhat overshadowed by TV. Although radio has the advantage of being relatively cheap and quick to produce, it has the obvious limitation of being restricted to sound, a major negative in the eyes of many marketers, who prefer to be able to show their product. Radio enthusiasts argue, however, that the visual element of a radio broadcast is supplied by the listener's imagination.

But the medium faces challenges. Subscription services such as Pandora, Spotify and satellite radio offer ad-free music, their growing popularity fuelled by consumers' irritation with the sheer quantity of radio commercials (the average US station runs nine minutes of ads per hour). In response, advertisers are increasing their use of live endorsements from the DJ, or the weather or traffic reporter, or 'embedding' their products into contest or chat segments – for example, a competition to win a holiday might involve a prize being provided by an airline, in return for several mentions on-air – with the result that consumers may not even be aware they are being advertised to. ∎

LEFT: Howard Stern, one of the most popular American radio presenters of today, moved in 2006 to subscription-based satellite radio service Sirius XM, whose music stations do not broadcast commercials.

OPPOSITE: Ovaltine, a children's drink, began broadcasting a radio show to the UK featuring a group of singing children called the Ovaltineys, in 1935. The show was so popular that by 1939, the Ovaltineys Club had attracted 5 million members.

# "We are the Ovaltineys"

OVALTINEYS are among the brightest and happiest of children. They know that 'Ovaltine' is a delicious appetizing drink and make it a golden rule to drink this nourishing beverage every day. It is delightful with any meal and is a favourite bedtime drink with thousands of Ovaltineys. It helps to keep them strong and full of energy.

**EVERY BOY AND GIRL SHOULD JOIN THE LEAGUE OF OVALTINEYS**

Members of the League of Ovaltineys have great fun with the secret high-signs, signals and code. Children can join the League and obtain their badge and the Official Rule Book (which also contains the words and music of the Ovaltiney songs) by sending a label from a tin of 'Ovaltine' with their full name, address and age to: THE CHIEF OVALTINEY (Dept. Q), 42 Upper Grosvenor Street, London, W.1.

*1/6, 2/9 and 5/- per tin.*

P.740A

ABOVE: *Practically every square inch of a racing car is covered by a sponsor's logo... as are the drivers' overalls.*

LEFT: *Confident that boxer Julius Francis would be knocked down in his fight with Mike Tyson, UK newspaper* The Mirror *sponsored the soles of Francis's boots.*

OPPOSITE: *Cadbury's sponsored every episode of the popular UK soap opera* Coronation Street *from 1996 – 2006.*

'*Brought to you by ...*'

IDEA № 30
# SPONSORSHIP

Although some members of the public believe sponsors are 'supporting' an event out of philanthropy, sponsorship is in reality a hard-headed commercial arrangement, designed to raise awareness, build brand loyalty and drive the company's bottom line.

Sponsorship was advertising's first method of broadcasting commercial messages through the fledgling radio stations in the 1920s – companies paid to have their name mentioned at the beginning and end of a show. In 1932, the Blackett-Sample-Hummert agency in Chicago extended the idea by actually creating a whole show – a female-targeted drama series – on behalf of one of their detergent clients. It was the first 'soap opera'.

The sponsorship practices of radio were simply carried over to TV when that medium took off in the US in the late 1940s: many successful early TV shows were known by their sponsors' names, such as the *United States Steel Hour*, and *Maxwell House Coffee Time*. Sometimes the sponsors exercised a great deal of control over the content of the show, even going so far as to have their ad agency create it. But sponsorship began to decline when TV and radio stations realized they could make more money by offering commercial messages in smaller time slots (30-second spots) and selling them to multiple businesses throughout their broadcasts, rather than selling sponsorship rights to one company for a whole show.

Sponsorship experienced a resurgence in the 1970s when cigarette brands were banned from TV advertising and turned their attention to sponsoring major sporting events instead, notably Formula 1 motor racing. And when the cost of TV commercials began to rise dramatically in the 1990s, advertisers again went looking for other ways to get their brands seen on TV, which led to a second wave of growth in sports sponsorship arrangements – to the point where, in some sports matches today, not only are the teams' shirts sponsored but also the stadium, the ball and even the referee. ∎

# *Desire beyond reason*

IDEA Nº 31
## SURREALISM

The Surrealists set out to shock, be noticed and to explore the nature of desire – no wonder their ideas had such an influence on advertising.

The term 'surrealist' was coined by French poet Guillaume Apollinaire in 1917, and it became the label of an artistic movement that believed in exploring the unconscious mind, the use of abstract and absurd imagery, and juxtaposing elements not normally found together to produce startling effects. As the popularity of surrealist artists such as Magritte and Dalí grew in the 1920s and 30s, big brands including Ford, Shell and Dubonnet were among those to employ surrealist techniques in their ad campaigns.

Surrealism was displaced by sentimentalism in the 1950s and realism in the 1960s, but it came back with a vengeance in the 1970s, where its oblique and allusive style proved especially influential in categories where product qualities could not legally be promoted, e.g. tobacco (which spawned the classic Benson & Hedges and Silk Cut campaigns in the UK) and alcohol.

Surrealist imagery has now been so widely used in advertising that it can veer towards cliché, such as marketers placing a 'light' beer, yoghurt or chocolate bar floating in the air – after Magritte, who placed a rock in the sky. And since surrealism gives licence to produce bizarre and unusual work, which offers an obvious appeal to creatives, it has at times been used self-indulgently, when such a treatment may not best serve the product or idea.

Yet at its core, surrealism has a huge relevance for advertising. Dalí's desire to 'astound' his audience conforms to Job 1 of an ad: get noticed. Another obvious parallel is that both surrealism and advertising make use of symbolic imagery to express and trigger our desires.

The incongruous juxtapositions, dark humour and irony of surrealism have undoubtedly influenced many well-known campaigns, from Cadbury's 'Gorilla', to Tango and Skittles, just as they influenced comedians such as Monty Python and the Mighty Boosh. And if nothing else, it is a classy way to exaggerate. ∎

ABOVE: *Magritte-influenced Ford poster, 1938.*

OPPOSITE BOTTOM: *Benson & Hedges ad, 1978, with surreal substitution of songbird for cigarette pack.*

RIGHT: *Dali-influenced imagery from Ogilvy Paris, for Perrier.*

'Both surrealism and advertising make use of symbolic imagery to express and trigger our desires.'

# As recommended by ...

## THE TESTIMONIAL

Nothing is more convincing than a member of the public telling us that they have tried a product and they love it. Only trouble is, consumers have started to question whether these so-called members of the public really are ...

Testimonials have been around since advertising first appeared in print. Their enduring popularity stems from a belief among advertisers that testimonials will make their products' claims more believable, since it is not the brand making them – which would be self-serving – but a third party, who is impartial. Hence the effectiveness of a testimonial is heavily dependent on whether the public does buy into the impartiality of that third party.

There are two main types of testimonial. The 'expert testimonial' comes from someone with credibility in the field, e.g. a nutritionist recommending a particular food product. The potential for scepticism is obvious – consumers know that the expert has been paid to appear in the ad. To counteract this, their performance needs to come across as sincere.

The 'average user' testimonial is delivered by a member of the public. Although not an expert, this person can convince if consumers feel that someone 'just like them' likes the product. It is normally apparent from their tone of voice, and the non-verbal cues they give off, that they are sincerely impressed by the brand. However, if their performance is too polished, the attempt can backfire, because consumers may believe they are an actor rather than a genuine member of the public.

In recent years, consumers have become more and more suspicious of these 'members of the public', and with good reason. When the Federal Trade Commission (FTC) launched an investigation into testimonials in US advertising, it found that an alarming number were fictitious. In 2009, the FTC introduced a new code of conduct for testimonials, to prevent consumers being misled. The issue is particularly acute online, with innumerable hotel and restaurant owners posting positive reviews about themselves, and many cases of bloggers failing to disclose that they have been paid to praise particular products. Since no foolproof method has yet been devised to verify that online testimonials are authentic, the problem of trust looks likely to become worse. ∎

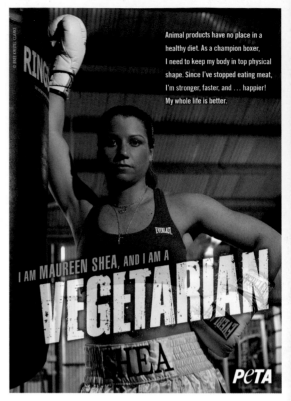

ABOVE: *The surprising testimonial – you would not expect a champion boxer to be a vegetarian.*

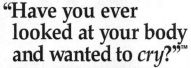

# "Have you ever looked at your body and wanted to *cry*?"™

*"Well, that's how I felt before I used Hydroxycut and lost an incredible **23 pounds!** Before I added Hydroxycut to my weight-loss program, I never thought I would ever be able to lose all this weight, especially after having children! Now, thanks to Hydroxycut, I've finally lost weight and I feel younger, energetic, and more beautiful than ever! If you **really** want to lose weight fast, you should use Hydroxycut."\**

— Brandi Carrier, Orlando, Fl

**BEFORE** **AFTER**

Lost **23** lbs!

Lost **19** inches!

Lost **8** dress sizes!

**BEFORE**

**AFTER**

*"Hydroxycut helped me lose weight where I needed it most – my butt and thighs."\**

*"I easily lost 23 pounds of ugly fat with Hydroxycut in just 8 weeks! Hydroxycut made me feel young and beautiful again."\**

Brandi's results not typical\*

Hydroxycut has quickly become one of the most *popular* weight-loss products for *men and women* all across America. It has been featured on commercial TV networks nationwide, and used by television actors, fashion models and thousands of people for one reason – it works! Hydroxycut is *clinically proven* and designed to deliver fast, natural weight loss. Hydroxycut also gives you the *energy boost* you need to make it through even the toughest day. Whether you need to lose a lot of weight or just those *last ten pounds*, nothing works like Hydroxycut! Try Hydroxycut for yourself today. You will be amazed with your results!\*

*"Hydroxycut is the single most effective, natural weight-loss product I've ever used. I highly recommend it to both men and women!"\**

— Dr. Christine Lydon, MD

*Hydroxycut is available at GNC and fine stores everywhere.*

Advanced Weight Loss Formula

**HYDROXYCUT**

Lose Fat *Fast!*
Increase Energy
Clinically Proven
100% Natural

Dietary Supplement

MUSCLETECH
Research And Development

**160 Capsules**

**GNC** LiveWell. Walgreens RITE AID

www.hydroxycut.com

ABOVE: *The expert testimonial – who better than a dentist to tell you what is best for your teeth?*

ABOVE: *Testimonial by a member of the public. Some consumers put more trust in 'ordinary people like me' than in experts.*

'In recent years consumers have become more and more suspicious of these "members of the public", and with good reason.'

# *Why say it when you can sing it?*

IDEA № 33
# THE JINGLE

The practice of setting advertising messages to music has a long history, but is now widely ridiculed – though far from extinct.

Jingles have been around since the beginning of commercial radio in the early 1920s. They became a powerful new selling-tool for advertisers: after all, the deliberately simple, repetitive, almost nursery rhyme-like messages do more than just *communicate* a product's name and benefits – the information gets stuck in your head.

The first jingle to become famous was 'Have you tried Wheaties?', which debuted in 1926, and turned a brand that was about to be discontinued into a nation-wide best-seller. Jingles grew steadily in popularity and became such an important technique that the creative director of London agency Allen Brady & Marsh kept a white grand piano in his office.

But by the 1980s, the phenomenon had begun to wear out. Audiences were more sophisticated, and the form had become a cliché. Agencies turned instead to pop music, such as Pepsi's use of Michael Jackson, and Nike's licensing of the Beatles song 'Revolution' in 1987. The rebellious climate of the 1960s and 1970s had given way to the commercialism of the 1980s, and pop stars were less reluctant to allow their music to be used for advertising – even tailored for advertising – which allowed jingles to evolve into branded re-workings of existing tracks, for example Jerry Lee Lewis's 'Whole Lotta Shakin' Goin' On' becoming 'Whole Lotta Breakfast Goin' On' for Burger King. (See also **No. 57, Pop Music in Ads**.)

Today, that technique too has become hackneyed, and yet the jingle has not completely disappeared. Companies may still use one if they want to be perceived as cheap, cheerful and unpretentious ('We buy any car, dot com'). Jingles are also becoming increasingly popular in a new, *wordless* form: keen to exploit the power of sound recognition, but recognizing that jingle lyrics have become cheesy, companies such as Intel, Audi and Philips have created short, purely melodic 'sonic brand triggers' to round off their communications. ∎

Twoallbeefpattiesspecialsaucelettuce-
cheesepicklesonionsonasesameseedbun

You just read the recipe for McDonald's
Big Mac sandwich. It starts with beef, of
course. Two lean 100% pure domestic beef
patties, including chuck, round and sirloin.
Then there's McDonald's special sauce, the
unique blend of mayonnaise, herbs, spices
and sweet pickle relish. Next come the
fresh lettuce, golden cheese, dill pickles and
chopped onion. And last, but far from least, a
freshly toasted, sesame seed bun. All these
good things add up to the one and only
taste of a great Big Mac.

**Quality you can taste. And trust.**  McDonald's

*ABOVE:* 'I'd like to teach the world to sing, in perfect harmony...' Coke song, 1971.

*OPPOSITE BOTTOM:* 'Two all-beef patties, special sauce, lettuce, cheese, pickles, onions on a sesame-seed bun!' The 'Big Mac Chant', first used 1974.

*RIGHT:* The famous Intel jingle, or 'sonic brand trigger'.

BUMMMM.     BUM - BUM - BUM - BUM.

## 'Jingles are becoming increasingly popular in a new, wordless form.'

# Brands become businesses

OPPOSITE: *Unilever builds its brands around different consumer needs. In the UK, Persil is sold as the 'family' washing liquid, while Surf's positioning is based around scent – the contrast between the two brands' homepages couldn't be clearer.*

BELOW: *Some of the many washing detergent brands sold by Procter & Gamble in North America, each targeting a different market segment. Cheer, for example, is the 'color expert', while Dreft is 'the first choice for mothers'.*

IDEA № 34
# BRAND MANAGERS

The early mass manufacturers had the mindset of 'producers', but gradually their thinking evolved beyond just pushing out their products into the marketplace, towards building brands that satisfy consumer needs.

It was not an overnight revolution, but the principles were first crystallized in a now-famous memo written on 13 May 1931 by Neil McElroy, a 27-year-old middle manager at Procter & Gamble (P&G). Harvard graduate McElroy was working on an advertising campaign for Camay soap, and was frustrated that not only was he competing with soaps from Lever and Palmolive, but also with Ivory – P&G's own flagship product. He argued that each brand should be targeted at *different* consumer markets, and that each should be managed by its own dedicated brand manager, supported by a dedicated brand team, devoted to thinking about every aspect of marketing it. And he went on to outline other ideas that today have become standard practice, emphasizing the importance of research, of training and of measuring the success of marketing efforts.

The changes, which were enthusiastically adopted by P&G, were incredibly far-reaching. First, it meant restructuring the company around its individual products rather than by disciplines such as sales or finance. And since each brand was to be run almost as a separate business, with decisions made at the brand level rather than by senior managers, it had the effect of decentralizing (and speeding up) the decision-making process.

There were very considerable consequences for advertising. If the brand team were working to create 'product differentiation', then advertising had to support that, and help to actively position the brand in the consumer's mind, not just trot out its product benefits. And if the job of brands was to satisfy consumers' needs, then the ad agency had an important role to play in helping the brand manager identify those needs, assisting with research and even with new product development.

P&G's move to organize their company around brand teams was widely emulated, and is still prevalent today in consumer-products companies over the world; in fact brand management as a business technique was perhaps the most significant innovation in marketing of the twentieth century. As for McElroy, he became the next CEO of Procter & Gamble, and interestingly, all of P&G's CEOs since have come up through brand management. ■

'If the job of brands was to satisfy consumers' needs,
then the ad agency had an important role to play.'

## The 'suits'

IDEA № 35
# ACCOUNT EXECUTIVES

The account executive has a challenging role – representing the agency's point of view to the client and, simultaneously, representing the client's point of view within the agency. The skills needed are marketing acumen, charm and toughness.

The account executive position was invented by J. Walter Thompson, who took over an agency called Carlton and Smith in 1877 and renamed it after himself. The company specialized in buying magazine space, and after achieving success in that area, began to offer creative services too. This led to the requirement for a single point of contact for the agency's clients, to help them access the right resources within the agency. Thus the 'account executive' was born, and changed advertising forever by putting businesspeople rather than creative or media experts in charge.

The rise of the 'suit' went hand in hand with the growing professionalization of the industry, but it did bring an unanticipated side effect: the hold of a

powerful 'account baron' over a client relationship could become so strong that if the account handler moved to another agency, they were able to take the account with them. For example, when Maurice Saatchi quit Saatchi & Saatchi to set up M&C Saatchi in 1995, Silk Cut cigarettes, Mirror Group newspapers and electrical retailer Dixons all moved across too.

Such an overtly personal decision would be extremely rare within today's modern business environment, but good client relationships are still vital, both for getting great work out and for paying the bills. Hence, although the creative director may often be the most charismatic figure within an agency, it is usually the senior account executive

who is the leader; in fact, it is highly unusual for an agency CEO to come from any background other than account handling.

In some ways, the account executive's responsibilities have narrowed in recent years, since strategy has become the province of the account planner, creatives now routinely present their own work and there are separate departments for finance and personnel. On the other hand, as more and more new advertising disciplines arise, such as digital and social media, the need for a person to marshal the agency's increasingly varied resources has become more important than ever. ■

TOP: J. Walter Thompson was the agency that invented the role of account executive and it is still renowned for its strong client relationships. The agency has worked with Unilever for 109 years, Kraft for 89 years, Kellogg's for more than 80 and Ford for 65.

LEFT: Robert Webber, as 'Juror #12' in the 1957 movie 12 Angry Men, played to one public stereotype of the advertising executive: wisecracking, superficial and people-pleasing.

OPPOSITE: Pete Campbell (Vincent Kartheiser) and Roger Sterling (John Slattery) in the TV series Mad Men represent the other side of the profession's public image: charming, but ruthless.

'It is highly unusual for an agency CEO to come from any background other than account handling.'

*Better than the programmes*

OPPOSITE TOP: *The record number of people to view a single TV spot was the 119.6 million who saw 'Miss Evelyn's Wild Ride', an ad in which two guys imagine a schoolteacher cutting loose in a silver Chevy Camaro, shown during the 2011 Super Bowl.*

OPPOSITE BOTTOM: *The most-awarded TV ad of all time, Honda 'Cog', by Wieden+Kennedy London, 2003.*

BELOW: *A still from the first TV commercial ever broadcast, for Bulova watches, 1941.*

IDEA № 36
# TELEVISION ADVERTISING

The first TV ads were black and white, rather static and very dull. But within a few years, the medium had evolved into the most powerful form of mass communication yet devised.

The first TV commercial aired on 1 July 1941, during a baseball game between the Brooklyn Dodgers and Philadelphia Phillies, at a time when there were only 7,500 TV sets in New York City. The ad was for Bulova watches and showed a watch-face superimposed over a map of the US, while a voiceover claimed that 'America runs on Bulova time'. The company paid $9 to run the ad.

In the early years of American TV, many shows had a single sponsor, such as the *Kraft Television Theater*, but by the late 1940s, the 30-second spot was becoming more popular. Most other countries had initially opted for a state-funded model, so their television stations did not at first carry any advertising. In the UK, for example, the first commercial was not broadcast until 1955; it was a 60-second ad for the Unilever-owned Gibbs SR toothpaste.

TV's most dominant period arguably came in the 1960s and 1970s, when there were fewer stations available, so advertisers could reach a huge percentage of the population with just a handful of spots. The power of the medium to engage audiences emotionally meant there was no more powerful brand-building technique than a TV ad, though conveying complex information is a task more suited to print or online executions. In recent years, the huge quantity of new digital and cable TV channels have fragmented the market, although by offering lower ad rates, they have enabled a broader range of advertisers to use TV as a medium.

TV advertising has faced many threats over the years, from zapping (the invention of the remote control lets viewers change channels when the ads come on) to zipping (fast-forwarding the ads with a TiVo-type device) to the rapid rise of the internet competing for ad dollars. And yet the medium is still growing. Partly this is because it has been able to innovate, offering new types of sponsorship opportunities and new formats, such as five-second 'break bumpers' or 'bookends', and even one-second blipverts. But partly it is simply because TV still works. ■

AMERICA RUNS ON BULOVA TIME

# *Probing the public*

IDEA № 37
# RESEARCH

Lord Leverhulme famously said 'I know that half my advertising doesn't work, I just don't know which half.' Research is an attempt to solve that problem and allow advertisers to make decisions based on data, not just intuition.

There are two main types of research – 'pre' and 'post'. 'Pre' research is conducted before an ad runs, often using rough stimulus material such as storyboards; it aims to get a read on whether the ad is likely to be effective, mostly by asking people whether they found it memorable or persuasive. 'Post' is conducted after a campaign has run.

Research can be conducted online, on the phone, in the street, in focus groups, or it can be gathered by looking at credit-card and loyalty-card data. 'Quant' (quantitative) research produces hard numbers, such as the percentage of people who recall seeing a particular ad campaign, whereas 'qual' (qualitative) delves more into people's thoughts and feelings about a product category, or a proposed commercial.

Formal research was first conducted in 1879 by the N. W. Ayer agency, in a pitch for the advertising business of Nichols-Shepard Co., a manufacturer of farm equipment. And it began as a separate industry of its own in 1911, when J. George Frederick set up the first specialized research company, with General Electric as his first client.

The industry grew modestly until a significant breakthrough in the 1950s, when George Gallup developed Day-After Recall, a method of measuring an ad's memorability, which is still in wide use today. As the cost of advertising increased in the 1960s, so did the pressure on marketers to ensure budgets were well spent, and the market-research industry boomed. From the 1970s, computers began to be used to conduct large-scale data analysis, though in recent years researchers have begun to challenge the traditional tenets of rational and data-based research, and are increasingly examining the effect that advertising has at an emotional level, which is held to be a better predictor of sales success than rational measures such as recall.

Despite the industry's rise to prominence, research has its detractors, who complain that ideas that are genuinely original tend to get shot down in a focus group setting because people feel more comfortable discussing the familiar than the novel. The Aeron chair, the Walkman, the ATM and *Seinfeld* all failed research. ∎

ABOVE: *Cadbury's 'Gorilla' ad received a low score for 'well-branded' in pre-testing. But following release, the ad achieved the highest-ever branded recall score – 96 per cent.*

'Ideas that are genuinely original tend to get shot down in a focus-group setting.'

# The unique selling proposition

IDEA № 38
## THE USP

American adman Rosser Reeves revolutionized the industry with his ruthless focus on communicating a product's 'unique selling proposition' (USP).

A belief in the power of unique claims was not new, and had been employed by admen such as Claude Hopkins with his early 1900s campaign for Schlitz beer that advertised its bottles were 'washed with live steam'. But it was Rosser Reeves, at the Ted Bates agency in the early 1950s, who was the first to give the idea a name, and express it in a coherent philosophy that gained widespread traction throughout the marketing world.

Once he had identified a product's USP – the single factor that made a product superior to its competitors – Reeves would usually encapsulate it in a slogan (such as 'Melts in your mouth, not in your hand' for M&M's) and then reinforce the point with a visual demonstration. Before Reeves's USP thinking became orthodoxy, advertisements often featured a 'laundry list' of product benefits, or made generic claims that other brands were also making.

Reeves's hard-nosed approach to creativity led to huge success for Ted Bates in the 1950s and early 1960s. His campaign for headache remedy Anacin, for example, was able to triple the product's sales.

However, Reeves's ads were often repetitive and irritating, since he aimed solely to make his USPs clear and memorable, and made no attempt to produce commercials with entertainment value. He famously asked 'Do you want fine writing? Do you want masterpieces? Or do you want to see the goddamned sales curve start moving up?'

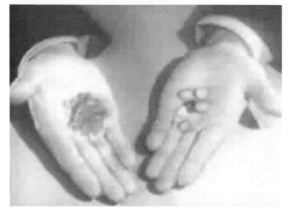

By the 1960s, Reeves's style was becoming less effective, as consumers began to reject heavy-handed sales messages and instead were responding to ads that were clever, interesting or funny. The ad industry's 'creative revolution' had begun, and in 1966, following a run of account losses, Rosser Reeves resigned from Ted Bates at the age of 55.

Nevertheless, a key tenet of Reeves's philosophy remains almost universally accepted today. Although there are now few products with a genuinely unique competitive advantage (see **No. 58, Product Parity**) – excepting the case of new inventions such as Dyson's bagless vacuum cleaner – almost the entire marketing industry has adopted Reeves's view that a product's advertising should focus on a single benefit. ∎

*ABOVE: Still from a 1950s commercial by Rosser Reeves, demonstrating the USP that M&M's chocolate 'Melts in your mouth, not in your hand'.*

*OPPOSITE: Dyson vacuums are bagless – a true USP. Or at least it was at the time of launch.*

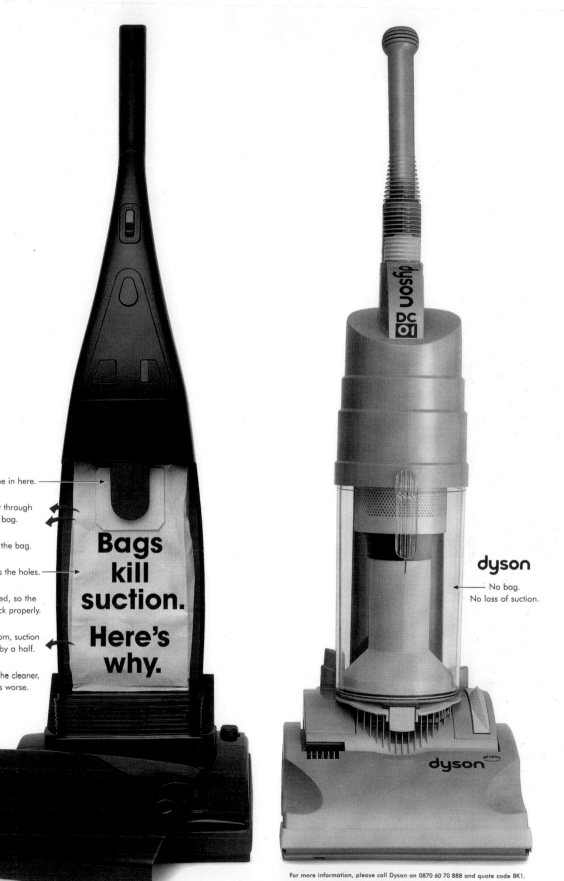

Air and dirt come in here.

The air goes out through
tiny holes in the bag.

The dirt stays in the bag.

But the dirt clogs the holes.

Airflow is reduced, so the
cleaner can't suck properly.

After just one room, suction
could be down by a half.

And as you use the cleaner,
the problem gets worse.

**Bags
kill
suction.**

**Here's
why.**

dyson

No bag.
No loss of suction.

For more information, please call Dyson on 0870 60 70 888 and quote code BK1.

ABOVE: *What to do when you realize you want to reach for the TV remote, but your hands are under a blanket? 26 million wearable blankets known as Snuggies® have been sold worldwide, thanks in large part to their infomercials.*

OPPOSITE TOP: *Poop-Freeze – subject of one of the most notorious infomercials on American TV.*

# *But wait ... there's more!*

IDEA № 39
## THE INFOMERCIAL

Though seemingly targeting insomniacs, and at times laughably crass ('Operators are standing by!'), infomercials generate serious revenues – over $150 billion in the US per year.

The forerunner of the infomercial was an hour-long television programme that viewers in San Diego received in the 1970s, advertising local homes for sale. It avoided the Federal Communications Commission (FCC) maximum 18 minutes of commercials an hour by broadcasting from Tijuana. The first infomercial for a consumer product aired in 1982, arranged by Chicago ad exec Frank Cannella for a hair-growth treatment.

The genre's distinctive style was developed by marketer Michael Walshe in a series of infomercials for Ginsu knives, which showed them miraculously slicing through tin cans. Ginsu knives were not miraculous – they were not even Japanese – but between 2 and 3 million Ginsu sets were sold in the early 1980s thanks to the application of 'hard sell' door-to-door sales techniques to television, such as adding a slew of small gifts to 'close the deal', with language sich as 'But wait ... there's more!', which has since become an infomercial staple.

The regulations for long-form paid programming vary by country – for example, until the early 1990s Canadian infomercials were required to consist only of photographs without moving video. The restriction was lifted as worldwide suspicions of the form began to recede.

Some products sold via infomercials appear laughable, including Poop-Freeze (to help clean up after your dog) or the UroClub, a discreet way to relieve yourself on the golf course. But others have become sales phenomena – such as home gym equipment, rotisserie cookers and the Tae Bo workout programme – and made stars of their pitch-men.

In recent years, the form has been adopted by politicians. A week before the US 2008 general election, presidential candidate Barack Obama bought a 30-minute slot during prime time on seven major TV networks to present a 'closing argument' to his campaign. The broadcast drew a peak audience of over 33 million viewers, making it the single most watched infomercial ever broadcast. ∎

IDEA № 40
# GRAPHIC DESIGN

Graphic design in an advertising context refers to the careful arrangement of text and imagery to ensure an ad can communicate its sales message effectively. Good graphic design gives an ad impact. And great graphic design can make an ad brilliant.

The term 'graphic design' first appeared in a 1922 essay titled 'New Kind of Printing Calls for New Design', by American designer William Addison Dwiggins. The call was warranted because although advertising had produced several examples of great design – Marius Rossillon's work featuring the Michelin Man that began in the 1890s, John Gilroy's Guinness series that began in the 1930s in the UK, and the wartime propaganda art of many nations in World War II – these were exceptions. The majority of ads were text-heavy and dull-looking.

The change finally came with a graphic-design revolution in New York in the 1950s, when designers such as Paul Rand, Saul Bass, Milton Glaser and George Lois began to produce logos and layouts with a boldness and modernity that completely shook up the staid world of advertising design. These members of the 'New York school' believed design should be arresting and provocative rather than polite and illustrative. They employed type and visual elements in a graphic and deliberately shocking manner, borrowing from the minimalist European aesthetic of the Bauhaus.

In the mid-1980s, the arrival of graphical software packages transformed the process of advertising design, speeding it up considerably and introducing thousands of new possibilities. Some complain that today's art directors and designers are lacking in traditional craft skills (such as drawing ability) but compared to the pre-digital age, almost every ad nowadays is at least competently designed, and there are multitudes – from the cool, clean look of an Apple print campaign to the visual dynamism of a Nike or Adidas poster – that are outstanding.

An increasingly important aspect of graphic design nowadays is 'interface design', which determines how a user will interact with a website or mobile site. Today's 'user experience' or UX designer is not just concerned with how design looks, but with the journey it creates. ∎

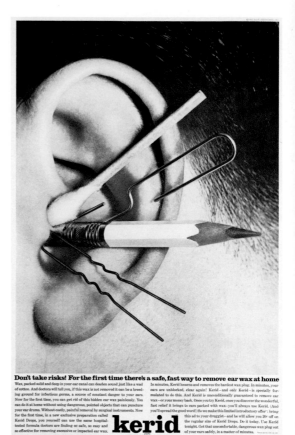

ABOVE: *Typically impactful design by George Lois in this ad for an ear wax treatment, 1959.*

A Fox is quick (0 to 50 in 10 seconds).
It's surefooted (front-wheel drive).
This sly, cunning sedan can take the
sharpest turns nimbly (sports car type
steering and suspension). It can
stop practically in its tracks
(power front disc brakes). And it doesn't
eat much (23 miles per gallon).
Best of all, for under $3,200* you
can catch the Fox.

YOUR HUNT IS OVER. THE QUICK, SLY, CRAFTY, CUNNING FOX BY AUDI IS HERE.

*Suggested Retail Price $3199 East Coast P.O.E. (West Coast slightly higher.) Price subject to change without notice. Local taxes and other dealer delivery charges, if any, additional.

ABOVE: *US ad for Audi, created by DDB
art director Helmut Krone and using
graphic designer Herb Lubalin's
Avant Garde typeface.*

'The majority of ads were text-heavy
and dull-looking.'

# Group creativity

RIGHT: *TV commercial from 2011 that depicts a 'trainstorming' session, with British musician Jarvis Cocker, French film director Michel Gondry and Belgian pop star Arno Hintjens discussing ideas for the opening ceremony of the London 2012 Olympics, while travelling on the Eurostar.*

OPPOSITE: *A key tenet of brainstorming is to focus on quantity – to literally throw lots of ideas at the wall.*

IDEA № 41
# THE BRAINSTORM

Brainstorming is a problem-solving method that involves gathering a group of people together and asking them to come up with as many ideas as they can.

Originally, advertising creativity was the province of 'a man on his own in a room'. Over time, ad agencies experimented with putting more people in the room. And today, group creativity sessions have become widespread – in some agencies, staff may attend a brainstorming session virtually every day of the week.

It was Alex Osborn – the 'O' in BBDO – who in 1942 published a book called *How to Think Up*, in which he first described the technique of brainstorming. The theory is that, in a group setting, people spark off each other and come up with more and better ideas than they would individually. Osborn set out two principles for brainstorming, which are still the cornerstones of the technique today. The first is to focus on quantity, from a belief that 'quantity breeds quality'. The second is that participants must not criticize others' ideas – this encourages people to share even their most radical-seeming thoughts.

More recent collaborative methodologies include Edward de Bono's *Six Thinking Hats* (1985), under which the brainstorming group cycles through a series of different thinking *styles* to solve a problem, and 'scrum' thinking, first used in 1993 in the US, in which a team adopts an iterative approach to speed up innovation.

Nevertheless, the classic brainstorm – often nowadays called a workshop – remains the most popular group creativity technique used by the ad industry. In fact, new technology has now been developed to facilitate brainstorming between participants in different offices or countries, via 'electronic brainstorming software' such as Monsoon.

This comes despite recent challenges concerning the method's efficacy. Researchers have found brainstorm participants are inhibited by a feeling that the lesser contributors in their group are 'free riding'. Another problem is 'evaluation apprehension', despite the ground rules of brainstorming explicitly stating that no idea is to be criticized. The phenomenon of 'blocking' may further reduce productivity – while one person is outlining an idea, the other participants are forced into listening mode, rather than thinking. And group productivity may itself be an illusion – is it really the case that a ten-person group comes up with more than ten times the ideas of ten individuals? ∎

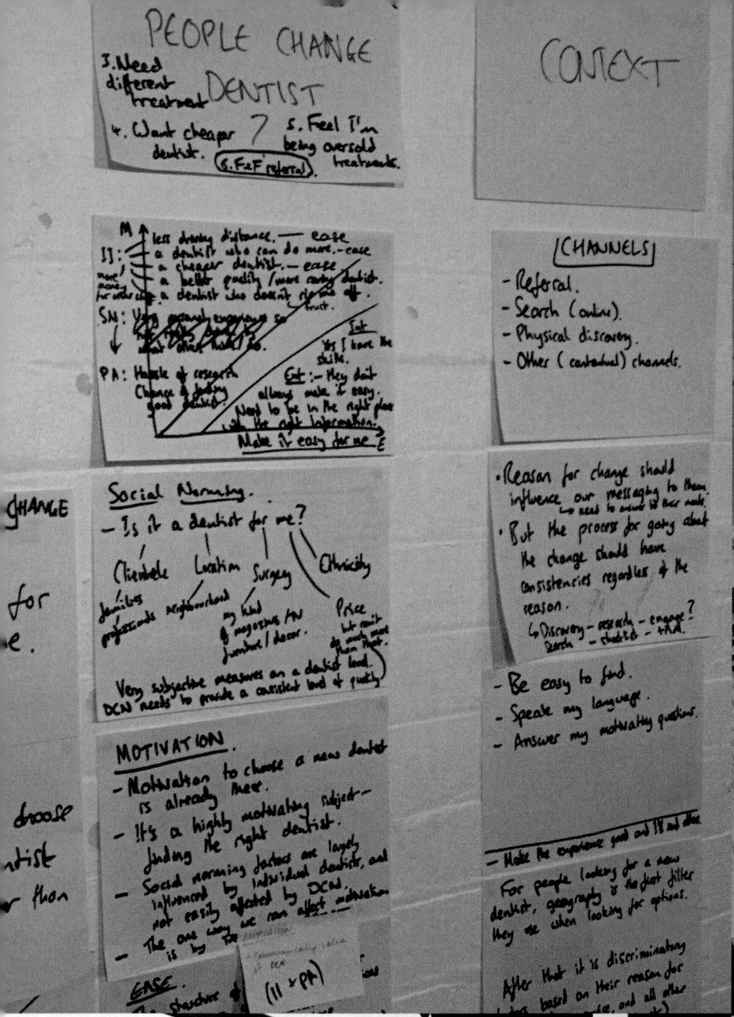

**PEOPLE CHANGE**

DENTIST

CONTEXT

3. Need different treatment
4. Want cheaper dentist. (6. F&F referral)
5. Feel I'm being oversold treatments.

**CHANNELS**
- Referral.
- Search (online).
- Physical discovery.
- Other (contextual) channels.

**Social Norming**
- Is it a dentist for me?
Clientele · Location · Surgery · Ethnicity

**MOTIVATION**
- Motivation to choose a new dentist is already there.
- It's a highly motivating subject — finding the right dentist.

**EASE**

- Reason for change should influence our messaging to them.
- But the process for going about the change should have consistencies regardless of the reason.
- Be easy to find.
- Speak my language.
- Answer my motivating questions.

---

RETAIL/InStore

OTHER

Anything Goes — PHILADELPHIA

MAY TRACES

On-pack

---

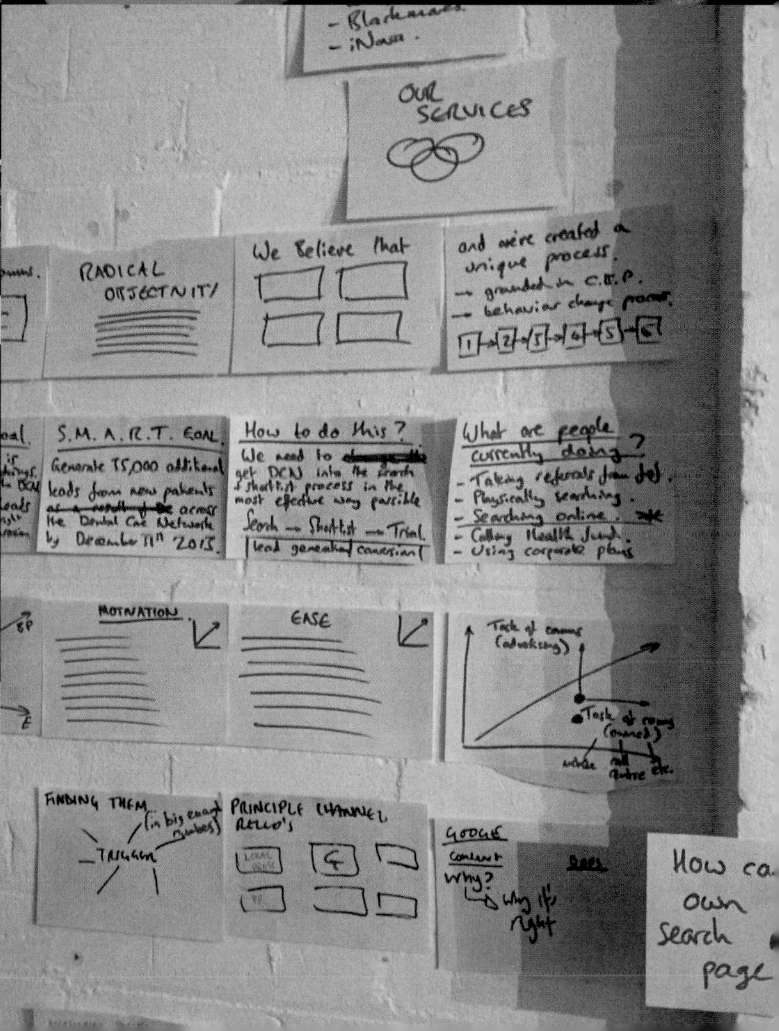

OUR SERVICES

RADICAL OBJECTIVITY

We Believe that

and we've created a unique process
→ grounded in C.B.P.
→ behaviour change process
1 2 3 4 5 6

**S.M.A.R.T. GOAL**
Generate 15,000 additional leads from new patients across the Dental Care Network by December 11th 2013.

**How to do this?**
We need to get DCN into the search shortlist process in the most effective way possible.
Search → Shortlist → Trial

**What are people currently doing?**
- Taking referrals from...
- Physically searching
- Searching online
- Calling Health Fund
- Using corporate plans

MOTIVATION

EASE

FINDING THEM

PRINCIPLE CHANNEL

GOOGLE
why? why it's right

How can own search page

*Cannes do*

# AWARDS

The advertising industry is obsessed with awards, perhaps because they are the only tangible gauge of an entirely subjective product – creativity.

The most important creative awards show is held in Cannes, in the south of France, in late June every year. It began in 1954 as a festival purely of cinema advertising; press and outdoor advertising were added in 1992, and cyber in 1998. Other notable awards schemes include the Clios, first awarded in 1960, and D&AD, which dates from 1963.

At Cannes – officially the Cannes Lions International Festival of Creativity – thousands of ads from all over the world are showcased, and judged by industry juries. In 2012, a record 34,301 entries were received, with the best of them being awarded a prestigious 'Cannes Lion'. Around 9,000 registered delegates from 90 countries visited, to celebrate the best of creativity – but also to network. Cannes is the only occasion when the entire worldwide industry comes together so, in addition to the awards it dishes out, the festival has become a forum where industry issues are discussed, new ideas are disseminated, important hirings conducted, even where clients are taken to be wooed.

But Cannes has its critics. Perhaps some are repelled by the 5AM ambience at the notorious 'Gutter Bar' on the Croisette. Others bemoan the behaviour of delegates at the awards shows, who do not hesitate to loudly 'whistle' any winners they feel are undeserving. The very notion of awards shows is condemned in certain quarters as a self-indulgent backslapping exercise. Some believe that awarding creativity rather than effectiveness undermines the industry's credibility in the eyes of marketers. And every awards show has been hit by scandals involving 'scam' or 'ghost' ads (see **No.73, Scam**).

Yet ad agencies seem happy to continue spending a fortune on flying their staff out to awards shows and entering their work for awards – to enter a TV ad at Cannes, for example, costs 640 EUR. Agencies feel the sums are worthwhile because winning awards may attract new clients. They also definitely help to recruit and retain talent, since creative people are often motivated by recognition, and therefore strongly prefer to work at the agencies that are winning awards. ∎

Awards ceremonies are held across the globe and for a variety of different sections of the industry, but the Cannes Lion (top right) remains the most prestigious creative award.

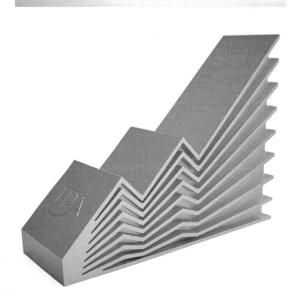

# Sellebrities

RIGHT: *Andrew Robertson, worldwide CEO of BBDO, is never seen without brightly coloured braces – he has taken the biggest stereotype of an adland wardrobe and made it his own.*

BELOW: *Trevor Beattie (bottom left), the most famous adman in the UK, whose unusual and engaging personality has generated as many column inches as his work has.*

## IDEA № 43
# THE PERSONAL BRAND

To sell an idea, ad agencies have to convince the client that this campaign will make their product famous. It certainly does not hurt if the person presenting the idea is a little bit famous themselves.

The early admen were anonymous – they let their work speak for itself. But when pioneers such as Claude Hopkins and Raymond Rubicam became well known within the industry, their fame attracted clients, and a celebrity arms-race began, with admen scrambling to write books and publish newspaper articles that would enhance their reputations.

In the early 1960s, David Ogilvy raised the bar to a new level – he became the first adman to achieve fame in the wider world, principally by writing two immensely popular books: *Confessions of an Advertising Man* in 1962 and *Ogilvy on Advertising* in 1983. Aside from being an advertising genius, Ogilvy had a genius for self-promotion. He was the original 'Englishman in New York', with his pipe, tweed suits and tea served every afternoon by a maid named Bridey Murphy. Ogilvy's fame undoubtedly helped drive the success of his agency, which grew from nothing to become a leading worldwide agency in just 12 years.

Today, every agency in the world makes efforts to build the personal brand of their principals by having them write articles for newspapers, appear on radio or TV shows, judge award shows or chair industry bodies.

It is perhaps easier for creatives to cultivate a personal brand, since their personality comes through in their work. English adman Trevor Beattie, for example, achieved fame as the creative force behind Wonderbra's 'Hello Boys' ad, and cemented his reputation with the 'FCUK' campaign for French Connection. Then the media began to pick up on his quirky personal style (Trevor only wears black and white clothing, he bought one of Michael Jackson's gloves at auction and has booked a ticket on Richard Branson's space mission).

For other departments such as planning, the individual's blog, book or Twitter stream have become tools to build reputations. For example, Jon Steel's book *Perfect Pitch: The Art of Selling Ideas and Winning New Business* (2006) elevated this already highly regarded planner to the status of a godfather of the planning world, and he has gone on to fill high-profile roles within the WPP network. ∎

David Ogilvy cultivated the 'upper-class gentleman' image, especially when it played well in America.

'Aside from being an advertising genius, Ogilvy had a genius for self-promotion.'

# An education in selling

IDEA Nº 44
## AD SCHOOL

Although education for professions such as law, engineering and medicine has been around for hundreds of years, the first course with the title of 'Advertising' only began in 1905, and was taught by W. R. Hotchkiss, advertising manager of the John Wanamaker Company, at New York University.

As the importance of advertising grew, so did the provision of courses, and by 1950 there were 43 American institutions offering advertising courses, usually as part of their journalism or marketing programmes. Today, approximately 150 US colleges and universities offer advertising education, of which over 40 offer graduate programmes. The courses are designed to prepare students to enter the advertising profession – as account handlers, planners or media specialists – and are often taught by former industry practitioners.

The growth in advertising education reflects an increasing professionalization of the industry, whose image has over the years been blighted by perceptions that it is staffed by chancers and charlatans. Professional qualifications are now commonplace in advertising around the world, although in many countries, such as the UK, the top agencies prefer to pluck their next generation of account handlers and planners from among the brightest graduates of the top universities – whatever their degree subject – rather than insisting their recruits have a degree in advertising.

Historically, the best preparation for entry into the creative side of advertising was thought to be an English degree (for copywriters) or an art school education (for art directors). But this philosophy was gradually displaced after the first specialist courses for advertising creatives began in 1961, with the foundation of the 'Watford Course' in the UK, which aimed to teach the importance of ideas, and not just craft skills. Attending one of these courses is nowadays by far the most common way to break into the business.

After a certain amount of industry criticism that the colleges were churning out students with identikit portfolios, most ad schools today are keen to emphasize that they teach a broad range of skills, including digital and social media. Miami Ad School claims to help its students become 'fame generators, trendsetters and game changers', and rather than be known as a 'portfolio school', styles itself 'The School of Pop Culture Engineering'. ■

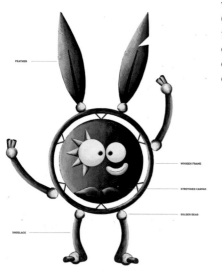

ABOVE: *This idea that featured a Toyota Tundra pulling the space shuttle Endeavor, which won four Gold Lions at Cannes in 2013, was created by a team at Saatchi & Saatchi LA that included art director Avery Oldfield and copywriter Adam Wolinsky, graduates of the VCU ad school in Virginia.*

OPPOSITE: *Idea for an animated character, by University of Ulster's Jonathan Mckee, which won a D&AD Student Award in 2011.*

LEFT: *The Miami Ad School has now expanded to 11 different locations, including Istanbul, Hamburg and Mumbai.*

'Miami Ad School claims to help its students become "fame generators, trendsetters and game changers".'

# The advertising that changed advertising

## IDEA № 45
# THE CREATIVE REVOLUTION

**Think small.**

Our little car isn't so much of a novelty any more.
A couple of dozen college kids don't try to squeeze inside it.
The guy at the gas station doesn't ask where the gas goes.
Nobody even stares at our shape.
In fact, some people who drive our little flivver don't even think 32 miles to the gallon is going any great guns.
Or using five pints of oil instead of five quarts.
Or never needing anti-freeze.
Or racking up 40,000 miles on a set of tires.
That's because once you get used to some of our economies, you don't even think about them any more.
Except when you squeeze into a small parking spot. Or renew your small insurance. Or pay a small repair bill.
Or trade in your old VW for a new one.
Think it over.

**Modern advertising truly began in 1949, when a New Yorker called Bill Bernbach started DDB – an agency whose creativity transformed the industry.**

Prior to DDB, many agencies focused on 'hard sell' techniques, using repetitive catchphrases, authority figures, diagrams and reams of information in their ads. The 'creative revolution', which gathered pace in the 1960s, instead used creativity and humour to generate attention and sales. It took its name from an essay written by Bill Bernbach titled *Manifesto for the Creative Revolution*, in which he urged that 'good taste, good art, and good writing can be good selling'.

DDB's ads were simple, honest and witty, and credited the reader with intelligence. Their uncluttered layouts took influences from the burgeoning field of graphic design and they employed a tone of voice that could be daringly self-depre-cating, such as 'Avis is only No.2 ... so we try harder', or a Volkswagen ad that described the car as a 'Lemon'.

DDB was also the first agency to put art directors and copywriters together to work as a team. Previously, a copywriter would write a headline and send the concept to the art department to be illustrated. Bill Bernbach's own experience of working with the supremely talented designer Paul Rand at the Weintraub agency in the 1940s led him to believe that an art director and copywriter working together would produce more powerful advertising, not only because the headline and art direction would be working in harmony, but because two creative individuals sparking off each other would create concepts more exciting than either could alone – a principle sometimes expressed as 1+1 = 3.

For a while DDB stood apart but, before long, the creative revolution began to spread. George Lois left DDB in 1960 to set up Papert Koenig Lois and Mary Wells spent seven years at DDB before starting Wells Rich Greene in 1966. In the UK, the baton was picked up by agencies such as CDP, BMP and Saatchi & Saatchi. Today, there is not an agency in the world that does not claim to put creativity at the heart of its offering. They all owe a debt to Bill Bernbach. ■

*ABOVE: The most iconic advertisement of the creative revolution – perhaps the century – by DDB for the Volkswagen Beetle; the art direction worked hand in hand with the lateral, witty headline.*

*OPPOSITE: Stills from recent Cannes Grand Prix-winning film* Carousel *for Philips by Tribal DDB Amsterdam.*

*BOTTOM LEFT: DDB was one of the first agencies to use non-white faces in its ads.*

**You don't have to be Jewish**

**to love Levy's**
*real Jewish Rye*

'DDB's ads were simple, honest, witty –
and credited the reader with intelligence.'

# Selling with a smile

BOTTOM LEFT: *John West Salmon 'Bear' ad, 2000, by Leo Burnett London, was given the title of 'Funniest Ad Of All Time' by* Adweek *magazine.*

IDEA № 46

# HUMOUR

Humour was first used in print ads in the mid-nineteenth century, in the form of limericks, cartoons and what was referred to as 'flippant copy'. But most early advertising practitioners *rejected* humour, preferring logical argument as a sales technique.

Humour, it was felt, would distract people from the sales message. And although there was a brief craze in the late 1920s for humorous cartoon-style advertising, most people in the industry agreed with David Ogilvy's famous dictum that 'Nobody buys from a clown'.

Nevertheless, use of humour did increase gradually from the 1930s onwards – influenced by the success of comedy shows on radio and TV – and finally exploded in the 'creative revolution' of the 1960s. New York agency DDB led the way, with humorous ads for Volkswagen, Levy's rye bread and Ohrbach's department store.

Initially, advertising humour stayed mostly within a narrow band of the comedy spectrum – the area commonly known as 'wit'. But over time it has expanded to include broad comedy, irony and dark humour. Today, humour is used in a large proportion of ads. Australia has the highest percentage of humorous TV ads (36 per cent), followed by the United Kingdom (33 per cent), the US (29 per cent) and China (25 per cent).

Recent research has proved David Ogilvy wrong – humorous advertising is in fact more likely to gain audience attention, increase memorability and enhance message persuasiveness. In categories that target young males, such as beer, it is almost essential. Even in the staid world of banking and insurance, humour can help give personality to an otherwise faceless institution. And visual humour is an effective tool to make ads work across multiple language markets.

Although enjoyment of humour is a universal human trait, it is also the case that humour is subjective, which inherently creates a risk – what one person finds hilarious may be lame or even offensive to others. When comedy goes wrong, the advertiser can suffer a backlash. But the paradox for marketers who decide to employ a low-risk, more conservative style of humour is that if the comedy does not push any boundaries at all, it is unlikely to work. ∎

'What one person finds hilarious may be lame or even offensive to others.'

## No.2 tries harder

IDEA № 47
# THE CHALLENGER BRAND

'Challenger brand' thinking states that a number 2 or 3 in a market needs to behave differently from the market leader – adopting a more competitive mindset, and a more challenging or quirky personality.

The original challenger brands were VW and Avis in the 1960s. When Volkswagen ran an ad with the headline 'Think small', it was challenging the conventional wisdom of the American car-buyer that bigger equals better. Avis based their entire ad campaign on the fact that they were No.2 in the market behind Hertz, arguing that this meant they had to try harder, and so offered better cars and better service.

Challenger brands may deliberately cultivate a more unusual personality than the typically 'safe' market leader. They can be mavericks (such as Red Bull), funsters (such as Virgin), a people's champion (Aldi) or can simply position themselves as a more modern alternative to the established player – Audi has had great success with this strategy in the US recently, urging consumers to 'escape the prison of old luxury'. By which they mean Mercedes et al.

The thinking behind the challenger-brand philosophy is that the most effective way for a smaller player to grow sales is to attack the market leader and to steal share by explaining why their brand is superior. So the Pepsi Challenge, for example, is rooted in the claim that Pepsi tastes better than Coke.

Conversely, it could be argued that the best strategy for the market leader is not to mention its competitors at all. First of all, attacking a smaller player can look mean-spirited. But also, since a majority of users already seem to prefer the market leader, the brand probably has more to gain by attracting new people into the category – perhaps by suggesting new usage occasions, or reminding people of the generic benefits of the category – than by putting efforts into strengthening its already-strong brand preference. ∎

open happiness™

*ABOVE: Coke follows the typical market-leader strategy and never attacks its challengers, but focuses on communicating the general benefit of the caffeinated fizzy drinks category – a refreshing lift to the mood.*

*BOTTOM LEFT: The longest-running of all challenger brand campaigns, the Pepsi Challenge began in 1975 and has been regularly revived ever since, most recently in 2011 in the American version of the X Factor.*

# Avis is only No.2 in rent a cars. So why go with us?

We try damned hard.

(When you're not the biggest, you have to.)

We just can't afford dirty ashtrays. Or half-empty gas tanks. Or worn wipers. Or unwashed cars. Or low tires. Or anything less than seat-adjusters that adjust. Heaters that heat. Defrosters that defrost.

Obviously, the thing we try hardest for is just to be nice. To start you out right with a new car, like a lively, super-torque Ford, and a pleasant smile. To know, say, where you get a good pastrami sandwich in Duluth.

Why?

Because we can't afford to take you for granted.

Go with us next time.

The line at our counter is shorter.

# Avis can't afford not to be nice.

Or not give you a new car like a lively, super-torque Ford, or not know a pastrami-on-rye place in Duluth.

Why?

When you're not the biggest in rent a cars, you have to try harder.

We do. We're only No.2.

*Avis ads by DDB, 1964.*

'Avis based their entire ad campaign on the fact that they were No.2 in the market.'

*Creative start-ups*

IDEA № 48
# THE HOT SHOP

When ad agencies grew into big businesses, it left a gap for start-ups – small, nimble and focused on doing highly creative rather than merely client-pleasing work.

In New York, these included DDB (founded in 1949), Papert Koenig Lois (1960) and Wells Rich Greene (1966). London produced Collett Dickenson Pearce (1960) and Saatchi & Saatchi (1970). The Saatchi brothers exemplified the 'hot shop' ethos. They were hungry for new business, to the extent of poaching other agencies' accounts, a practice frowned upon at the time. Keen to project an image of success, they reportedly paid actors to mill around their office to make it look busy when new business prospects visited. And of course, their creative work was thrillingly bold and modern. By 1986, Saatchi & Saatchi had become the world's largest ad agency, and could surely no longer be deemed a hot shop. Neither could DDB, which had a total of 54 offices in 19 countries.

But only a tiny minority of hot shops reach global status. Most implode. Some, such as BBH and Wieden+Kennedy, have deliberately limited their growth, setting themselves up as 'micro-networks' (see **No. 74, The Micro-Network**). But the fate of many successful hot shops is to be bought by a big network agency, seeking an injection of creative heat. A buyout not only brings wealth to the shop's founders, but often a new challenge – that of running a big agency – since the network acquirer is often deliberately buying a new management team as much as a new agency.

In recent years, much of the innovation in the advertising industry has come from hot shops. The idea to eliminate the account-handling function came from Mother (founded 1996) and KesselsKramer (also 1996); digital advertising was first mastered by start-ups such as Razorfish (1995) and AKQA (2001); media neutrality was championed by Naked (2000); and crowdsourced advertising was pioneered by Victors & Spoils in 2009.

Occasionally, the term hot shop is used in a derogatory fashion – large clients may deride an agency as 'just a creative hot shop', implying they have no serious brand-building capability. But other multinational clients have embraced the concept. For example, Adidas asked the small Dutch agency 180 Amsterdam to create its global advertising, and the TBWA network to distribute it. ∎

*What do you think of my accent?*

NOW EVEN MORE DOGSHIT IN THE MAIN ENTRANCE

Hans Brinker Budget Hotel Amsterdam ☎ 31 20 6220687

## 'Who' a brand is

**Archetype: the Everyman.**

IDEA № 49

# BRAND PERSONALITY THEORY

Successful brands have a 'personality', in a similar way to how people do. Helping to define and shape this personality has become an essential role played by ad agencies.

**Archetype: the Ruler.**

**Red Bull®**

ENERGY DRINK

**Archetype: the Explorer.**

Marketers had long known that consumers imputed human qualities to their brands, but a rigorous theory of brand personality was first set out in a paper called 'What Is a Brand?' written by Stephen King, Planning Director at JWT London, in 1971. King recommended that advertisers deliberately build their brands around human personality traits, so as to make them more appealing to consumers.

Today, it seems obvious that having a personality that consumers relate to will make a brand more successful, especially if the personality embodies characteristics that are desirable in that market, such as the 'everyman' qualities of Miller beer. Consumers also use brands for self-expression, and a brand with a clear and strong personality enables the consumer to make a clear statement about themselves. For example, there can be little doubt that its 'rugged' persona helped make Marlboro the world's most successful cigarette brand.

King's theory grew steadily in popularity until it gained near-universal acceptance. One of its applications is to ensure consistency in brand communications. For example, if Harley-Davidson

were to decide (as seems likely) that their brand personality is 'The Outlaw', the concept would act as a guiding framework for their various ad agencies in creating their advertising. The theory also assists marketers in creating differentiation for their brands, since a personality can help a brand stand out from its competitors, and may create a sustainable competitive advantage, because while it is easy to copy a product, it is harder to copy a personality. It can also guide product development, by judging whether a proposed new brand extension 'fits' with the brand's personality.

One popular set of human facets by which to view brands was developed by Jennifer Aaker of Stanford University in 1997, who defined the five 'core dimensions' of brand personality as excitement, sincerity, ruggedness, competence and sophistication. A more recent trend is to borrow theories of personality originating from psychology and philosophy. For example, Carl Jung developed 12 personality 'archetypes' – such as the Jester, the Sage, the Warrior – that are widely used today by advertising agencies as a means to help clients define their brands. ∎

*OPPOSITE TOP: UK smoothie brand Innocent promotes the idea that to be 'innocent' is to be honest, natural and engaging. These brand personalities are expressed in every aspect of the company's communications, including its packaging.*

*OPPOSITE BOTTOM: A graphic guide to brand archetypes.*

'While it is easy to copy a product,
it is harder to copy a personality.'

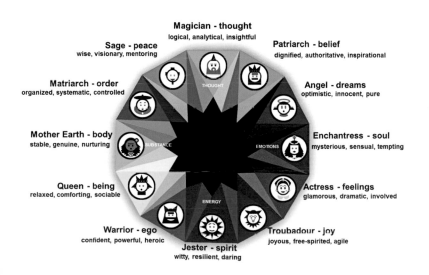

Magician - thought
logical, analytical, insightful

Sage - peace
wise, visionary, mentoring

Patriarch - belief
dignified, authoritative, inspirational

Matriarch - order
organized, systematic, controlled

Angel - dreams
optimistic, innocent, pure

Mother Earth - body
stable, genuine, nurturing

Enchantress - soul
mysterious, sensual, tempting

Queen - being
relaxed, comforting, sociable

Actress - feelings
glamorous, dramatic, involved

Warrior - ego
confident, powerful, heroic

Troubadour - joy
joyous, free-spirited, agile

Jester - spirit
witty, resilient, daring

THOUGHT

SUBSTANCE

EMOTIONS

ENERGY

# Accentuate the negative

*OPPOSITE: Saatchi & Saatchi introduced negative political advertising in the UK. Their 'Labour Isn't Working' and 'Labour Still Isn't Working' posters were widely credited with helping Margaret Thatcher come to power in 1979.*

*OPPOSITE BOTTOM: This example from the 2013 Israeli election campaign features an image of candidate Naftali Bennett, with the words 'Bennett is irresponsible; he supports insubordination'.*

*BOTTOM: Attack ads are now circulated on the internet and via social media. This one featured on the Daily Kos political website in 2012.*

IDEA № 50

# THE POLITICAL ATTACK AD

Attack ads rose to prominence in the US in the 1960s, and have since become a staple (and controversial) tool of modern political campaigning.

The most famous political attack ad – known as 'Daisy Girl' – features a little girl innocently counting as she removes the petals from a flower, until the sound of her voice is swamped by an ominous male 'countdown' voiceover, and the camera zooms in to an extreme close-up of the girl's pupil before cutting to footage of a nuclear explosion. This shocking and disturbing ad was produced for Lyndon B. Johnson's 1964 presidential campaign and played on fears that Johnson's opponent, the stridently anti-communist senator Barry Goldwater, could lead America into a nuclear war with the Soviet Union.

The Johnson campaign bought only one paid spot for 'Daisy Girl'; it only needed to air once, since it was immediately picked up and re-broadcast repeatedly by the news and current affairs programmes. Although the ad was criticized for using scare tactics, its power and success (Johnson won a crushing victory) ushered in a new era of negative political advertising.

George H. Bush severely damaged his opponent Michael Dukakis in the 1988 presidential election with hard-hitting attack ads, one of which – 'Willie Horton' – related the story of a jailed murderer who committed assault, theft and rape after being given a weekend pass in a programme supported by Governor Dukakis.

Sometimes attack ads backfire. In the 1993 Canadian federal election, an ad for the Progressive Conservative Party (PCP) attacked Liberal Party leader Jean Chrétien, while appearing to mock his medical condition (Chrétien was suffering from Bell's palsy, which causes partial facial paralysis). The resulting outrage is believed to have gone against the PCP in the polls.

But although voters – when asked – profess a dislike for attack ads, sophisticated research studies have found that negative political advertising does deliver positive results. ∎

It's 3 a.m. Who takes the call?

Put all foreign bases on alert. Get Joint Chiefs, SecDef, and NSA Director to the Situation Room in 15. Keep me informed.

Short GM – heck, dump all my U.S. industrials! Sell dollars, buy gold. Tight lid on this one! Don't panic the markets until I'm out!

'Sometimes attack ads backfire.'

# PUT A TIGER IN YOUR TANK

## NEW POWER-FORMULA ESSO EXTRA BOOSTS POWER THREE WAYS...

**1. QUICK STARTING.** New Esso Extra gives quick starting, in summer and winter, and *smooth controlled power* with that extra acceleration when you need it.
**2. SMOOTH FIRING.** Esso Extra's new Power formula improves ignition, helps your engine to fire smoothly and efficiently.

**3. HIGH QUALITY.** New Esso Extra has the high quality that modern cars need for peak performance. *So call at the Esso sign and fill up with new Esso Extra —and feel the difference.* PUT A TIGER IN YOUR TANK.

*Happy Motoring!* **Esso**

*Esso's 'Put A Tiger In Your Tank' campaign appeared in print, on TV... even on wall-clocks.*

# Multimedia marketing

Fine tune your morning.
got milk?

IDEA № 51
# CAMPAIGNS

An advertising campaign is a series of messages that share a single theme, which can run across different media over a period of months or even years – and which is far more effective than a sequence of unrelated ads.

Since the earliest days of mass-market print advertising in the nineteenth century, brands had run 'series' of ads. But it was not until the 1960s that advertisers began to fully exploit the power of integrated campaigns in different media channels. One of the earliest examples was a brand-awareness campaign for Esso petrol (now Exxon in the US) built around the theme of 'Put a Tiger in Your Tank'. The campaign, which launched in 1959, employed a suite of television, radio and print ads, plus competitions encouraging drivers to attach a fake tiger tail to their cars, promotional events featuring real tigers and tiger-striped gas-pump hoses. It was a huge success.

Today, a campaign that hits consumers at 'multiple touch-points' has become standard. Although there is extra expense in creating ads in all the various different media, the brand impression is vastly strengthened by being delivered via different senses, e.g. visual, auditory and tactile. Multiple executions also help prevent wear-out, and keep the brand story fresh. Budweiser's 'Whassup?' campaign, for example, which began with a group of young guys using the phrase, evolved many times – from showing an alien returning to his home planet and whose report about life on earth consisted of bellowing 'Whassup?', to an ad that depicted New Jersey wiseguys replacing 'Whassup?' with 'Howyoudoin?'

However, coming up with an idea that can work successfully across multiple media is considerably more difficult than coming up with one-off ideas. And with the proliferation of media channels in recent years, it is argued that brands can become guilty of 'surrounding' the consumer – bombarding them with their campaign message wherever they go, becoming an unwelcome presence in their lives. And in their determination to execute broad-based campaigns, brands can fall into the trap of simply 'turning up' in every media channel, without truly engaging the consumer.

Hence today there is a minor backlash against traditional campaign thinking, with brands increasingly looking to drive deeper engagement rather than just greater breadth. Given the possibilities of the internet to create more immersive experiences, using game-like or storytelling mechanisms, the 'other media' may no longer be true expressions of a campaign theme, but instead play the role of driving consumers to a website, or an online film. ∎

# Doing the right thing

# PRINCIPLES

For the majority of its existence, advertising displayed a woeful absence of ethics. The industry's view was that its role was to serve the client, not to make moral judgements.

Hence the nineteenth century saw heavy advertising of patent medicines, although they patently did not work. That only came to an end when the publishing industry, not the ad industry, began to ban these 'quack' medicine ads, in 1892.

The general opinion of the industry's moral standards has always been low, fuelled by books such as Frederic Wakeman's 1946 novel *The Hucksters* and Vance Packard's *The Hidden Persuaders*, published in 1957, which (falsely) alleged that advertising made use of subliminal messaging, and played on people's unconscious fears to sell products.

Meanwhile, admen themselves have either been seen as sleazy – inhabiting the louche world of the TV series *Mad Men* – or as having a 'bend with the wind' morality, epitomized by the spineless adman character in the movie *12 Angry Men* (1957). (See also **No. 67, Advertising as Fiction**)

But gradually, admen with principles began to appear. In 1964, Emerson Foote shocked Madison Avenue when he resigned from his position as chairman of McCann-Erickson, saying, 'I will not have anything to do with any advertising agency which promotes the sale of cigarettes.' Foote's announcement came eight months after the release of the landmark Surgeon General's report on the link between smoking tobacco and lung cancer.

DDB New York even dropped an encyclopaedia client who had been marketing their product to children when Bill Bernbach decreed it was too complicated for children. And in Britain, David Abbott – founder of what is today the country's largest agency, Abbott Mead Vickers BBDO – famously refused to work on cigarette or toy accounts.

The industry's conscience has today well and truly awakened. The new standard-bearer is Alex Bogusky, founder of US agency Crispin, Porter + Bogusky, who left the agency in 2010 and is now spearheading an organization called Common, which seeks to raise awareness of social and environmental issues – tagline 'Do shit that matters'. ∎

TOP RIGHT: *Some agencies are now refusing to take on fast-food accounts. They question the industry's use of toy give-aways to appeal to children, given the increasing prevalence of childhood obesity.*

LEFT: *Many ad agencies now do* pro bono *work on behalf of not-for-profit organizations, such as this print ad for Reporters Without Borders by BETC Paris.*

OPPOSITE: *Camel cigarettes ad, 1946.*

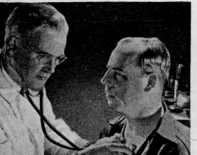

*Every doctor in private practice was asked:*
—family physicians, surgeons, specialists…
doctors in every branch of medicine—
*"What cigarette do you smoke?"*

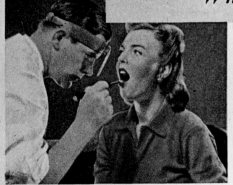

*According to a recent Nationwide survey:*

# More Doctors Smoke Camels

*than any other cigarette!*

**THE "T-ZONE" TEST WILL TELL YOU**

The "T-Zone"—T for taste and T for throat—is your own laboratory, your proving ground, for any cigarette. For only your taste and your throat can decide which cigarette tastes best to *you*…and how it affects your throat. On the basis of the experience of many, many millions of smokers, we believe Camels will suit your "T-Zone" to a "T."

**CAMEL** — TURKISH & DOMESTIC BLEND CIGARETTES — CHOICE QUALITY

Not a guess, not just a trend…but an *actual fact* based on the statements of doctors themselves to 3 nationally known independent research organizations.

Yes, your doctor was asked…along with thousands and thousands of other doctors from Maine to California.

And they've named their choice—the brand that more doctors named as their smoke is *Camel!* Three nationally known independent research organizations found this to be a fact.

Nothing unusual about it. Doctors smoke for pleasure just like the rest of us. They appreciate, just as you, a mildness that's cool and easy on the throat. They too enjoy the full, rich flavor of expertly blended costlier tobaccos. And they named Camels…more of them named Camels than any other brand. Next time you buy cigarettes, try Camels.

# *Advertising opens up*

IDEA № 53
# DEMOCRATIZATION

The 1960s saw an influx of admen from the wrong side of the tracks who gave advertising a jolt of creativity and energy.

Up until the 1950s, American advertising was a staid profession, whose staff had a similar background to lawyers or bankers. People from non-WASP backgrounds were excluded, sometimes explicitly – Jews, for example, found it difficult to enter the business because many clients openly refused to have them on their accounts. And Jerry Della Femina, who later founded his own successful agency, was told in an interview at JWT that 'on the basis of your name alone, Ford wouldn't want you working on their business'.

But the late 1950s was the era of rock and roll, the teenager and the beat poets. Society was changing fast. Jewish writers, musicians and film-makers were coming to prominence – they could not be kept out of advertising forever. Many got their break at DDB. Bill Bernbach did not care about

ethnicity or race, only talent. Many of Bernbach's creatives were Jewish, George Lois was Greek, Phyllis Robinson and Mary Wells were female, and it seemed that all the art directors were Italian. However, it has to be stated that the doors had not yet fully opened for African-Americans, who by 1967 represented only 3.5 per cent of ad agency employees, and are still under-represented today, at 5.3 per cent of the total advertising population.

In Britain, the barrier was class. Advertising had been a gentleman's profession and in the 1950s many agencies were staffed by ex-army officers. The 1960s saw the business open up – in tandem with the social changes taking place in 'Swinging London' that allowed working-class talents to break through in music, art, fashion and photography. Working-class creatives such as Geoff Seymour and Alan Parker at Collett Dickenson Pearce began producing incredibly fresh work. Whereas previously advertising had been largely 'aspirational', their honest but heartwarming depictions of ordinary life, for brands including Hovis and Birds Eye, charmed the nation.

But despite these advances, advertising still has a long way to go. Worldwide, the industry still suffers from a lack of diversity, with ethnic minorities and women under-represented, especially at the highest levels (see **No. 28, Women in the Workplace**). ∎

ABOVE: The 'Miracle Stain' 2013 Super Bowl ad for Tide featured a black couple as the central protagonists, a sign of the increasing democratization of casting in US commercials.

OPPOSITE: DDB New York was one of the first mainstream agencies to hire Jewish copywriters and therefore a natural choice to do the advertising for El Al, the national airline of Israel.

RIGHT: 'Ben' ad for Birds Eye®, directed by Alan Parker in 1974 – one of the first on British TV to feature ordinary working-class people.

# Advertising gets serious

IDEA № 54
# PROFESSIONALIZATION

Advertising has evolved from a Wild West business, populated by charlatans and failed poets with debauched habits and a notoriously slack work ethic, into what today is a professional and respectable industry – albeit slightly less fun to work in.

From its earliest days, when it was purely a media-sales business, advertising has had a slightly disreputable image. This is perhaps not surprising, as it is a business that requires no capital, no qualifications except the gift of the gab, and its pricing can be opaque and results hard to quantify. Then when agencies began to add creative services in the second half of the nineteenth century, they opened their doors to all kinds of renegades; successful creatives often seemed to be people who had failed at 'normal' jobs.

There have always been a few notable exceptions – advertising executives who have achieved success partly by *standing out* from the fast-and-loose crowd, such as J. Walter Thompson (known as 'The Commodore'), Claude Hopkins of the Lord & Thomas agency (who in 1923 wrote a book called *Scientific Advertising*) and uber-creative revolutionary Bill Bernbach, who was known for being a non-smoking, moderate-drinking family man.

But once advertising began its long boom period, fuelled by the huge profits made from the growth of TV advertising, the business entered the era depicted in the TV series *Mad Men*, with a culture of heavy drinking, drug-taking and sexual licence. French adman Jacques Séguéla (the 'S' in Euro RSCG) even titled his autobiography 'Don't tell my mother I work in advertising, she thinks I play piano in a brothel'. (See also **No.67, Advertising as Fiction**.)

However, the early-1990s recession curbed some of the excesses. Clients began to demand greater transparency on agency costs, and appointed procurement managers to scrutinize every budget. Agency incomes tumbled with the dotcom crash of 2000, forcing greater efficiency and professionalization, such as electronic timesheets. Email and smartphones have created an 'always on', instant-response culture. Increased use of research, technology and data has signalled a general shift away from agencies relying on instinct and artistry towards placing a greater focus on results and effectiveness.

Today's ad-landers are themselves a new breed: in digital media, many have come from technical backgrounds rather than the more traditional arts education; advertising has also recruited more specialists with genuine professional qualifications, in areas such as consumer psychology and data planning; and in general, there are more people in advertising today who have actually studied marketing or advertising at college and are committed to a career in the industry, whereas in the past they were often people who had 'ended up' in it. ∎

ABOVE: *Jacques Séguéla's autobiography, its English title is* Don't tell my mother I work in advertising, she thinks I play piano in a brothel.

BOTTOM LEFT: *Claude Hopkins took advertising seriously.*

OPPOSITE: Mad Men's *'Roger Sterling' ... drink in hand.*

'Successful creatives often seemed to be people who had failed at "normal" jobs.'

ABOVE: *Rather than trying to compete with the athletic credentials of Nike and Adidas, which would have required exorbitant media spending, Droga5 has cleverly repositioned Puma as the brand for the 'after hours athlete'.*

LEFT: *Some clever planner has refined the expression of the Cadbury's brand down to a single word: Joy.*

## The brains of the outfit

IDEA № 55
# ACCOUNT PLANNING

**The main role of the account planner is to help an agency create advertising that truly connects with consumers.**

Advertising agencies had always carried out consumer research for their clients, but the researcher would usually present his findings and then disappear. In London in 1968, both Stephen King at JWT and Stanley Pollitt at BMP had the idea of bringing the researcher into the *heart* of the advertising process, working alongside the account managers and creatives.

The change was every bit as significant as Bill Bernbach's move to pair copywriters with art directors. A good planner can create more insightful briefs for the creatives – and then help explain to the client why their work is right, since it is based on sound research, and not just gut feel.

The popularity of account planning grew rapidly in the UK, though it took a little longer to be adopted in other markets. Jay Chiat imported the idea to the US in 1982; other agencies took note after watching Chiat\Day grow from billings of $50 million to $700 million in ten years.

Today, there are account planners in every large agency, and they fulfil several functions. First, they help define the task that the advertising must achieve. Secondly, they collate information about the consumer and the market, perhaps spending time with consumers using the product, or with focus groups, asking them what they think about the product and the category. This information feeds into the writing of a brief for the creatives, the centrepiece of which is the planner's strategy – the means by which the communications will solve the brand's problem. Planners are also heavily involved in creative development, to ensure that the work being produced will resonate with consumers, and are often involved in presenting to the client, outlining how consumers are likely to react to the advertising. Finally, the planner will evaluate the success of the agency's last round of advertising ... and then the cycle begins again. ■

RIGHT: *The power of strategy: in 1985, Lucozade changed course from 'The drink for when you're sick' ('Lucozade aids recovery') to being a sports drink ('Lucozade replaces lost energy') in a campaign featuring Olympic decathlon champion Daley Thompson. Sales tripled in five years.*

# *Shooting stars*

IDEA № 56
# SUPERSTAR DIRECTORS

TV advertising began in 1941 and for its first 30 years was visually sterile. Many ads used spokesmen speaking straight to camera, or simple animation.

Even during the 'creative revolution' of the 1960s, despite some witty and charming ads for Volkswagen, there were no TV commercials produced that were anything like as creatively interesting as what was happening in the cinema. But as the advertising environment became more cluttered, marketers realized they had to make their work stand out, which gave directors the licence to make more distinctive-looking spots.

In the US, Joe Pytka and Joe Sedelmaier (see **No.61, Interesting Casting**) introduced a completely new style of ad in the early 1970s – with faster editing, more unusual casting and bravura visual comedy – perfectly suiting the 30-second format. In the UK, Ridley Scott's 'Boy on a Bike' commercial for Hovis (1973) broke new ground in its filmic cinematography and mastery of the audience's emotions.

Through the 1980s and 1990s, TV budgets rose stratospherically, and as agencies produced increasingly epic and special-effects-laden commercials, the role of the director took on ever-greater importance, with the very top directors able to command upwards of $25,000 a day.

In many cases they are worth it. Ever since Alan Parker and Ridley Scott broke through to directing movies, the previously unregarded world of commercials has attracted talented people hoping to follow in their footsteps. Directors such as Tarsem, Tony Kaye, Michel Gondry, Spike Jonze, Jonathan Glazer and Rupert Sanders all cut their teeth on commercials and, in fact, still make

them. Despite the limitations imposed by the need to sell a product, directors are attracted by the high budgets in advertising (many multiples per second of a movie budget) and the opportunity to experiment. For example, it was for a Smirnoff commercial in 1998 that Michel Gondry invented the 'bullet time' effect, later used in *The Matrix*. ∎

ABOVE: *2013 Audi commercial directed by Jonathan Glazer, whose movie credits include* Sexy Beast *(2000) and* Birth *(2004).*

OPPOSITE: *The iconic Hovis 'Boy on a Bike' ad, directed by Ridley Scott.*

**Hovis** AS GOOD FOR YOU TODAY AS ITS ALWAYS BEEN!

# As heard on TV

# POP MUSIC IN ADS

Until the 1980s, the music in TV ads was either a jingle, incidental music or a classical piece. Pop stars were not willing to let their records be used for commercials – this was viewed as 'selling out'.

But once the 'political' atmosphere of the 1960s and 70s gave way to the commercialism of the 80s, the flood-gates opened. A watershed moment was Nike's licensing of The Beatles song 'Revolution' in 1987. The Beatles had sold their publishing to a third party, but nevertheless, the appearance of The Beatles on a commercial made the idea seem suddenly acceptable. And when bands saw how much money was on offer – the Rolling Stones licensed 'Start Me Up' to Microsoft in 1995 for a fee reported as anything from $3–8 million – final resistance crumbled.

In fact the situation soon reversed, with record companies queuing up to have their music featured on ads, because a popular commercial could lead to a huge bump in an artist's sales. For example, no fewer than *seven* tracks went to No.1 in the UK following an appearance on a Levi's ad – including the Clash's only UK No.1.

The advantage for advertisers of using existing music is the ability to choose a track that conveys exactly the right mood for their ad, or whose lyrics have exactly the right meaning. For example, Chevrolet's use of Bob Seger's 'Like A Rock' perfectly expresses what the company wants to say about its trucks.

Occasionally, the original meaning of the song is ignored by the advertiser. For example, Iggy Pop's 'Lust For Life', a song about taking heroin, is used to advertise Royal Caribbean cruise ships.

The high point of commercial pop-music licensing was the feeding frenzy around Moby's album *Play* in 1999 – all 18 of its tracks were licensed for commercials, some of them several times over. But today, with TV ad budgets becoming tighter, advertisers are using less music by well-known acts. They are turning instead to cutting-edge electronic music, or up-and-coming bands. ■

ABOVE: *In 2004, Apple licensed the U2 track 'Vertigo' as part of a sophisticated cross-promotion that also involved the release of a U2-branded iPod.*

OPPOSITE: *Tracks from the album* Play *by Moby were used in ads for an enormous array of products across Europe and the US (Moby shown opposite).*

# *Advertising as the differentiating feature*

IDEA № 58
# PRODUCT PARITY

In many categories, there is no real difference nowadays between rival brands. Thus the job of advertising has changed from communicating product differences to creating a *perception* of difference where in fact there is none.

Of course, many successful brands *have* been built on innovation, or a competitive advantage. In 1898, Uneeda Biscuits were the first to come pre-packaged rather than sold from a barrel. In 1948, Polaroid introduced the first instant camera. And in 1985, when Volkswagen's German engineering gave them an advantage in reliability, they introduced what became their famous UK tagline: 'If only everything in life was as reliable as a Volkswagen.' But over time, innovations are copied and differences erode. Now, all biscuits come packaged, all cameras take instant pictures and Volkswagen were forced to withdraw their slogan once nearly every car brand offered good reliability.

In fact, with manufacturing lead times becoming ever shorter, any advantage that a manufacturer is able to incorporate into their product tends to be eliminated in a matter of months, or even weeks, and therefore cannot be used as a long-term brand platform. Yet in a world of product parity, advertising arguably has become *more* crucial, since it can be used to create *perceived* difference. For example, Sony's 'Colour Like No Other' campaign, which began in 2005, successfully increased the market share of Sony TVs by creating a perception that Sony TVs had better colour, rather than communicating any real product difference.

The most extreme example of the phenomenon is found in categories such as tea, beer, fuel and aspirin, in which the competing brands are virtually iden-

tical (except for their packaging). A famous research study in 1990 showed that consumers in the UK strongly preferred (and were willing to pay a price premium for) PG Tips tea over supermarket own (store) brands, even though in blind taste tests they were unable to tell the difference. PG Tips had for many years run a popular advertising campaign featuring comical chimps, and since consumers had no genuine preference for the tea, one can only conclude they were 'drinking the advertising.' ∎

If only everything in life was as reliable as a Volkswagen.

'Over time, innovations are copied and differences erode.'

*ABOVE: The original PG Tips-drinking chimps.*

*LEFT: Consumers are prepared to pay a significant premium for Nike-branded sportswear over socks and shirts that are virtually identical, but unbranded.*

*OPPOSITE: 1987 Volkswagen Golf ad in which an angrily disappointed woman throws away her fur coat and her jewellery, but not her car keys, illustrating the tagline 'If only everything in life was as reliable as a Volkswagen.'*

OPPOSITE: *In its heyday, MTV was arguably operating as an advertiser-funded channel, playing three-minute ads for record companies' products 24 hours a day.*

*Brand as broadcaster*

IDEA Nº 59

# ADVERTISER-FUNDED CHANNELS

Historically, brands reached the public by paying to sponsor broadcasters' programmes, or placing ads around them. Now, however, brands are becoming broadcasters themselves.

The growth of cable and satellite TV in the 1970s dramatically lowered the cost of broadcasting, and enabled hundreds of new specialist channels to emerge, devoted to sport, music, motor cars, or even advertising (the programming of stations such as QVC and the Home Shopping Network consists of wall-to-wall commercials, albeit performed live). Arguably, MTV is another example, since the pop videos it plays are in fact all adverts for a product – the music track.

Following a relaxation of broadcasting regulations, individual companies were allowed to set up their own TV channels in the UK, and the first to begin broadcasting was the Audi Channel in 2005, with content such as celebrity test drives, behind-the-scenes features on how the cars are made, and motorsport coverage. Although the channel cost Audi a considerable amount of money to set up and maintain, it was deemed a success in terms of brochure and test-drive requests, and brand-engagement measures. After broadcasting for four years, the Audi Channel migrated to the internet.

Since the introduction of YouTube in 2005 (see **No. 96, YouTube**), every brand can become a broadcaster, since every brand can create its own YouTube channel. The cost of broadcast is zero, and some marketers have achieved good success from it – Walmart's YouTube channel, for example, has attracted 21 million video views and the Starbucks channel, 11 million. Not only is a YouTube channel a cost-effective way to communicate with consumers, it is also a useful tool for keeping the company's own staff informed and engaged.

Today there are a multitude of ways for brands to distribute their own content, rather than relying on traditional broadcasters and publishers. Magazine brand *Grazia* runs its own Grazia TV station on its website, and numerous brands push out content via video-on-demand and to mobile devices. Brands are also becoming their own publishers, presenting regular bursts of written content on their websites or on Facebook. ∎

ABOVE: *Rugby World Cup-winner Will Greenwood takes an Audi A4 for a spin around Munich, in a feature broadcast on the Audi Channel.*

LEFT: *The Walmart channel on YouTube.*

# The emotional selling proposition

## IDEA № 60
# THE ESP

The theory of the unique selling proposition (USP) dominated advertising thinking from the 1940s, until agencies began to realize that people actually buy for *emotional* rather than rational reasons – hence the coining of the term 'ESP'.

The importance of emotion as a driver of human behaviour was studied extensively by psychologists in the 1980s, and the idea then filtered through into the ad industry. The research showed that our decisions tend to be based on emotion – we only use logic to back them up, or explain them to other people. Therefore while it may *appear* that purchases are rationally driven, since a consumer may tell his friends (or a researcher) that he bought a particular car because of its build quality or low depreciation, the reality may be that he bought it because it makes him feel powerful, or successful.

Even in overtly rational categories, such as IT services, emotional considerations may still be paramount. This may

partially have accounted for the success of IBM – a head of IT may have chosen IBM because they unconsciously wished to align themselves with values such as success and solidity.

Even a wholly rational selling-point becomes more powerful if expressed with emotion. For example, a famous IKEA TV ad communicated a functional 'low price' message, by dramatizing the illicit thrill a woman felt when she exited the store with her bargains, urging her husband to 'Start the engine!'

However, the primacy of the emotions has not yet been fully accepted by marketers, many of whom – perhaps the majority – still prefer to focus on the rational. This is despite the fact that, ironically, there are sound rational

reasons for using an ESP. First of all, buyers who base their purchasing decisions on rational factors such as price alone, are often disloyal. Secondly, the era of product parity means that few brands actually possess a rational USP nowadays (see **No. 58, Product Parity**). And thirdly, a focus on the emotional triggers to purchase is being increasingly vindicated by neuro-scientific research, which has revealed that the parts of the brain we use when considering purchase decisions are indeed areas associated with the emotions. ∎

TOP RIGHT: *Patek Philippe's campaign constructs a sophisticated emotional sell rooted in the feelings of fathers for their sons.*

LEFT: *Mercedes is a brand that is rich in emotional associations – it almost never runs wholly rational advertising.*

*Raw emotion in this poster for Nike featuring England footballer Wayne Rooney in 'warrior' pose, 2006.*

'Our decisions tend to be based on emotion.'

# Making use of talent

IDEA № 61
# INTERESTING CASTING

After more than 100 years of hiring physically perfect individuals to represent their brands, advertisers began to realize they could achieve more impact by casting 'real' or unusual-looking people.

Advertising spent a long time constructing a fantasy world, populated by happy, square-jawed people. But in the 1960s, that approach began to seem hackneyed. In the US, ad directors such as Joe Sedelmaier and Joe Pytka began using non-actors in their commercials, who brought quirkiness and relatability to their spots. In the UK, Alan Parker and Ridley Scott were also using ordinary people, often with rarely heard working-class or regional accents, for greater realism and cut-through.

Perhaps the most famous example of the 'real people' approach to casting came in 1984, when Sedelmaier asked 81-year-old manicurist Clara Peller to demand 'Where's the beef?' in an ad for Wendy's. The line became a massive catchphrase across America, and made a cult star of the diminutive Peller. Meanwhile, Wendy's sales jumped 31 per cent in a year.

Gradually the bar for 'interestingness' rose higher, until by the 1990s it seemed that advertisers were no longer looking for 'real', but highly abnormal people. Renowned ad director Frank Budgen once told a scout finding him talent for a Stella Artois ad, 'Unless the face is extraordinary, I do not want it.' Another director is said to have conducted a casting session in a psychiatric hospital.

But since a primary goal is to make an ad stand out, as soon as any style of casting becomes an established trend, agencies and directors need to move away from it. Thus the fashion for extreme casting gave way to other approaches such as realism, celebrities cast against type, hipsters and minority ethnic groups.

The one type of person it is rare to see in an ad today is someone ordinary-looking. The accepted principle is that a commercial actor only has 30 seconds to make an impression, which means they need to be a 'bigger character' than a typical TV actor, more exaggerated in their performance style, and probably more unusual-looking. ∎

LEFT: *Iggy Pop makes an unusual (and memorable) choice of spokesperson for an insurance brand.*

# "Unless the face is extraordinary I do not want it."

ABOVE: *The UK ads for Stella Artois have a long history of extremely quirky casting.*

RIGHT: *Clara Peller became a cult hit for Wendy's; sometimes a non-actor gives a performance that no actor ever could.*

# Advertising's Super Bowl

IDEA № 62
# THE EVENT AD

The unusually large audiences that tune in for certain one-off live events – the Super Bowl in the US, and the *X Factor* final in the UK – have created a new type of ad: the 'event ad'.

The audience fragmentation caused by the arrival of new cable and satellite TV stations in the 1970s meant that the few big-audience shows that remained – such as the Super Bowl – became more important to advertisers, the cost of advertising in them became more expensive, and brands began to realize they had to produce ads with a scale and excitement to match the event itself.

An early example came in 1973, when Master Lock spent almost their entire annual marketing budget on a single ad that ran in the Super Bowl; it showed one of their locks surviving being hit by a rifle bullet. But the ad that defined the new paradigm was Apple's '1984' commercial. Directed by Ridley Scott, the dystopian mini-masterpiece was broadcast during Super Bowl XVIII, on 22 January 1984. In strictly economic terms, the media strategy did not make sense – having spent a near-record $900,000 on the production of the ad, Apple aired it only once. But the commercial garnered millions of dollars worth of free publicity, and was re-broadcast several times by news programmes – there was no need to run it again, and the fact that it only aired once gave it a 'special event' feel.

Today it is a common strategy for brands to make a commercial specifically for the Super Bowl; the ads are almost as eagerly anticipated as the game – and as heavily dissected afterwards. The average cost of a 30-second commercial during the 2012 Super Bowl was $3.5 million – an increase of $500,000 from the year before. The rise of social media is perceived to have made a Super Bowl (or *X Factor*) spot even more valuable, since viewers who are discussing the event will often also post about the ads, thus amplifying their reach. ∎

ABOVE: *The annual appearance of a highly emotive Christmas ad for UK retailer John Lewis has become an event in its own right. This 2011 iteration made its debut in top-rating TV show X Factor.*

RIGHT: *Nike's 'Write the Future' blockbuster, directed by Mexican film-maker Alejandro González Iñárritu, first aired on TV during the 2010 Champions League Final – in 32 countries around the world simultaneously.*

OPPOSITE: *Taco Bell's 'Viva Young' commercial was the most-watched ad of the 2013 Super Bowl.*

'The ads are almost as eagerly anticipated as the game.'

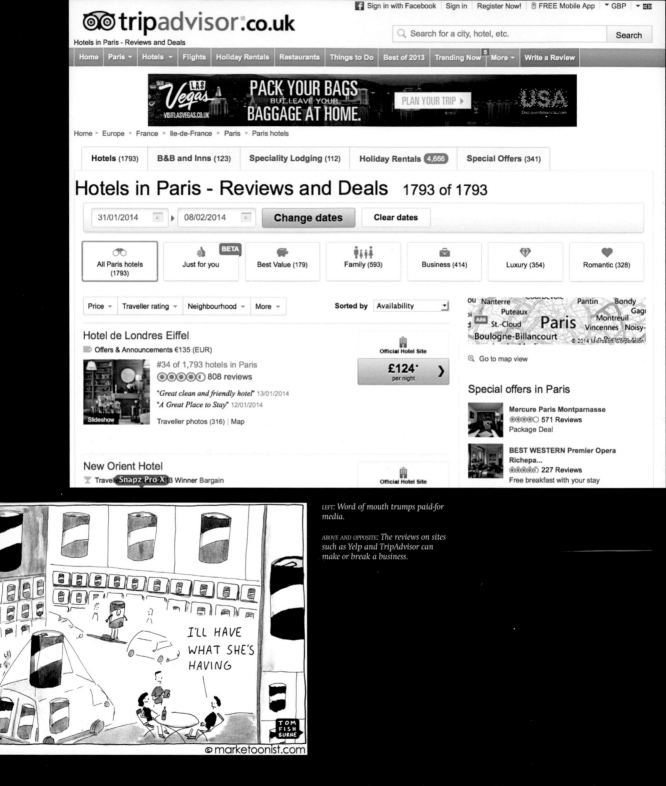

LEFT: *Word of mouth trumps paid-for media.*

ABOVE AND OPPOSITE: *The reviews on sites such as Yelp and TripAdvisor can make or break a business.*

'Ironically, the perception that online reviews are unbiased is exactly what has made marketers so determined to influence them.'

# *Recommends from friends*

IDEA № 63
# WORD OF MOUTH

In a sense, word of mouth is the oldest form of advertising – an ancient Babylonian, on discovering a pleasant tavern, would surely have told his friends about it. But since the true definition of advertising is 'paid-for communications', it did not strictly count until the recent emergence of *paid-for* word of mouth, now a fast-growing option for advertisers.

The goal of word-of-mouth advertising is to encourage consumers to talk about a brand or – better still – recommend it to others. An early example were the 'peer influence groups' put together in the 1970s in the US, when pharmaceutical marketers would arrange focus groups of physicians in which one or two were already fans of a particular drug, and would hence sway the others. And in the 1990s, there were occasional cases of brands paying influencers – such as taxi drivers – to talk positively about their products to consumers.

But the medium really took off with the arrival of Web 2.0, which enabled consumers to discuss and review products online. These reviews can reach hundreds or even thousands of people, many more than a traditional word-of-mouth recommendation would reach in the non-virtual world. And since individuals place a far greater trust in the opinions of their friends – or even strangers – than in communications self-interestedly paid for by brand owners, word of mouth in the form of online reviews has become a key driver of purchase in many categories, such as cars, holidays and restaurant meals.

Ironically, the perception that online reviews are unbiased is exactly what has made marketers so determined to influence them, for example by paying influential bloggers to test their products, a process sometimes known as 'buzz marketing'. Hotel and restaurant owners are now routinely paying for freelance writers to post positive reviews of their businesses – even if they have never visited them. Review sites such as Yelp and TripAdvisor claim they have sophisticated algorithms to detect phony postings, but the suspicion remains that many reviews on these sites are not genuine.

Word of mouth has also become a big consideration for 'traditional' media – marketers are keen to create ads that have talkability, since if an ad is talked about over a beer, or shared via social media, its effect can be multiplied many times over. ∎

*Products so good, they sell themselves*

IDEA № 64
# NOT ADVERTISING

Arguably, advertising is a kind of tax paid by companies who make unremarkable products, since exceptional products do not need advertising.

The Hershey Chocolate Company did not advertise at all before 1970; founder Milton Hershey said 'Give them quality. That's the best advertising in the world.' The idea is gaining ground today, with many companies deliberately taking the decision to invest their resources in improving their product or service, instead of in advertising.

But only very few companies, usually those founded on innovation, have a product which is genuinely unique or superior. Google's patented search algorithm has crushed all competitors, enabling the company to build a dominant position without advertising. However, Google's aversion to self-promotion ended abruptly in 2010, with a Super Bowl ad. Google CEO Eric Schmidt admitted 'Hell has indeed frozen over'. The move was possibly in response to competition from new

search engine Bing. In a completely different field, fast-growing lingerie brand Spanx has not yet advertised, relying instead on PR, word of mouth and a uniquely effective product.

Brands that have truly strong values sometimes do not need advertising to communicate them. The Body Shop, for example, was imbued with the spirit of its founder, Anita Roddick, whose commitment to social and environmental change acted as a beacon for customers; the Body Shop had never even had a marketing department before it went public in 1984. Ben & Jerry's does plenty of advertising nowadays, but for many years its founders' sense of fun and generosity made the company remarkable enough on their own.

Some companies, such as Ferrari, deliberately do not advertise because they want to foster a sense of exclusivity.

Brands that are in the connections business are able to get their users themselves to recruit new users, e.g. Facebook and Zynga and LinkedIn. And Costco has become the world's seventh-largest retailer with a no-frills, low-price strategy which is reinforced by the fact that they do not 'waste' money on advertising. ∎

*Spanx (top right) and Ferrari (opposite). Neither brand has ever advertised.*

LEFT: *Facebook acquired a billion users without spending a cent on advertising. Its first ad, 'Chairs', debuted in 2012.*

'Some companies deliberately do not advertise because they want to foster a sense of exclusivity.'

*Easily decoded symbolism, in this magazine ad for Gucci.*

www.gucci.com

# Symbols for sale

## IDEA № 65
## SEMIOTICS

Semiotics is the study of the *symbolic* meaning of words and objects. And since advertising is always aiming to make ordinary consumer products stand for profoundly desirable values, many marketers have become aware of the importance of ensuring that an ad conveys 'the right semiotics'.

Both Plato and Aristotle explored symbolism, as did John Locke in the seventeenth century, but it was in the 1950s that an awareness of the power of semiotics in advertising came to the fore. An influential 1955 paper by American marketing professor Sidney Levy outlined how advertising makes frequent use of symbolism, such as red colours to denote excitement, and theatrical references to imply glamour.

Roland Barthes, in his book *Mythologies*, published in 1957, also studied advertising from a semiotic point of view. He claimed that advertising is effective because it attaches products to cultural myths within our society. In other words, it is not just what a product does, but the meaning it has in the culture. For example, at a time when men feel their masculinity to be under threat, a beer may successfully be sold on the basis that it makes a man feel more manly. Vance Packard's *The Hidden Persuaders*, also published in 1957, examined advertising's use of symbolism too, but saw it as a sinister exercise in subconscious manipulation.

It is certainly true that consumers are very good at picking up on even quite subtle visual cues in an advertisement, which can signify which social class a product is being aimed at, and whether it is good value or high quality, stands for modernity or tradition, health or indulgence.

Symbolic values can also be communicated by words. For example, the name of the car brand Acura encodes 'precision', as well as a vaguely Italian sense of elegance.

Today, many marketers commission psychological 'depth studies' to unearth the codes of their brand or category. For example, although McDonald's overt advertising is about food, its marketers understand that part of what McDonald's 'means' to people is 'security': it is viewed as a safe, clean, family-friendly place, where the menu is predictable and comforting. Hence the marketers are careful to develop advertising concepts that play to this value. ∎

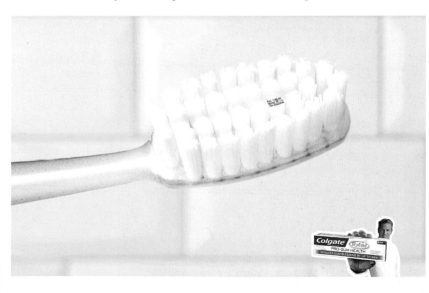

*TOP RIGHT: The halo symbolizes purity – an important 'code' of the vodka category.*

*LEFT: Ads for 'cleanliness' products, such as toothpaste, are often dominated by the colour white.*

*Covering advertising*

IDEA № 66
# THE TRADE PRESS

Almost every industry has one or more publications aimed at the people working within it – known as 'the trade press' – and advertising is no exception.

The world's first advertising trade magazine was *Printers' Ink*, founded in New York in 1888. For the first time, advertising staffers could gain a sense of what was happening in the industry as a whole, not just their own company. Suddenly a vast array of information had become widely available – from stories about people and accounts on the move, to the dissemination of new creative ideas.

A second vital function of the trade press is to provide a forum for debate. As far back as 1908, one Earnest Elmo Calkins wrote a column in *Printers' Ink* deriding the 'lifeless dummies that appear in magazine pages and upon posters', and recommended a more realistic style of advertising illustration. In recent years, the trade press has moved the industry forward by hosting debates in crucial areas such as the representation of minorities and women, and the ethics of advertising tobacco and alcohol (see **No. 52, Principles**).

*Printers' Ink* folded in 1967, but the US now has two major titles: *Advertising Age* (known as *Ad Age*) which was founded in 1930 and *Adweek* (1978). The UK is dominated by a single trade publication – *Campaign*. The latter was struggling until the late 1960s, when it was given a rebrand by Maurice Saatchi, with a striking new design, and became an immediate success. Other notable advertising trade titles include *AdVantage* (South Africa), *Propmark* (*Propaganda & Marketing*; Brazil), *Yes!* (Russia) and *Stratégies* (France).

Like the rest of the publishing industry, the advertising trade press has added internet editions in recent years, and many publications have begun sending out daily email updates to their subscribers, considerably accelerating the news cycle.

The negligible barriers to entry for online publishing have also enabled hundreds of advertising blogs to spring up. *Adweek* has *Adfreak*, and *Ad Age* publishes *Creativity*, but many are run by industry professionals, or even wannabes, as a hobby. In times past, a good ad might not be seen outside its home market until the following year's Cannes festival. But today it will be seen (and critiqued) globally, within a few hours of release, on websites such as *Ads of the World*. ■

ABOVE: *Michael Heseltine, who once challenged Margaret Thatcher for the leadership of Britain's Conservative Party, founded Haymarket, publisher of the UK's ad industry trade mag Campaign.*

BOTTOM LEFT: Printers' Ink, *the world's first advertising trade magazine, was founded in New York in 1888.*

*A selection of some of the world's leading advertising trade magazines*

*Novel settings*

# ADVERTISING AS FICTION

The advertising business has become a frequent setting for books and films, where it is usually depicted as a dishonest but entertaining way to earn a living.

The first novels set in the world of advertising began to appear at the start of the twentieth century and, from the beginning, dealt with problems of ethics. Samuel Hopkins Adams's *The Clarion* (1914) explored the falsehood of patent-medicine advertising, while Frederic Wakeman's *The Hucksters* (1946) and Sloan Wilson's *The Man in the Gray Flannel Suit* (1955) – which both also became movies – examined the corrupting effects of advertising's role as a servant of big business.

The proposed solution to the iniquities of advertising is sometimes for the hero to escape to the countryside, as in Shepherd Mead's *The Admen* (1958) and

Peter Mayle's *A Year In Provence* (1989), sometimes to quit writing copy and start tackling proper literature, as in Hartford Powel Jr's *The Virgin Queene* (1928) and George Orwell's *Keep The Aspidistra Flying* (1936), and sometimes for the hero to set up an agency of their own, which will produce only highly ethical or highly creative advertising, as in Harold Livingston's *The Detroiters* (1958) and Peter Carey's *Bliss* (1981).

Since the creative revolution of the 1960s, another perception of advertising has arisen – that it is a business that demands so much creativity, it can drive its practitioners insane. Examples include movies such as 1989's *How to Get*

*Ahead in Advertising*, in which Richard E. Grant believes he is growing a second head, and *Crazy People* (1990), in which Dudley Moore sets up an advertising agency in a lunatic asylum.

And yet the main effect of these fictional assaults on the meaninglessness, craziness and supposed deceptiveness of the industry has been to glamourize it, and inspire more people to want to work in it. In the same way that the behaviour of real-life mobsters is said to have been influenced by the TV show *The Sopranos*, there is little doubt that many in the ad industry enjoy comparing their lives to the characters and dialogue from *Mad Men*. ■

*LEFT: Mel Gibson and Helen Hunt played warring/dating ad execs in* What Women Want *(2000).*

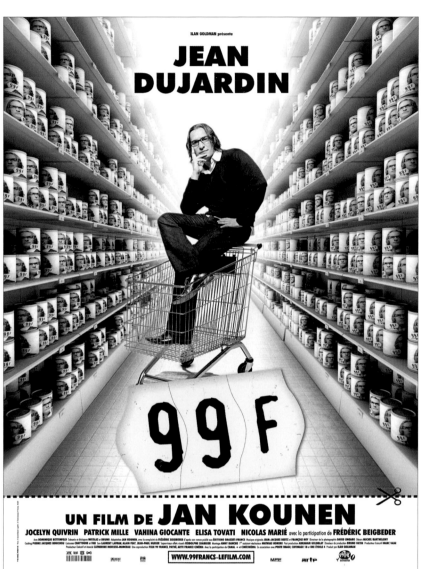

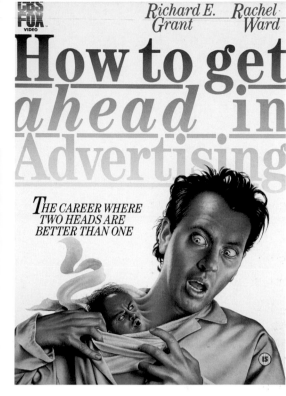

*ABOVE: The central farce in the 1989
movie* How to Get Ahead in
Advertising *involves Richard E.
Grant's advertising executive growing
a second head.*

*LEFT:* 99 Francs *(2000) by Frédéric
Beigbeder, a caustic novel set in the
French advertising industry, was
adapted into a film in 2007 starring
Jean Dujardin.*

'A business that demands so much creativity
it can drive its practitioners insane.'

# Advertising under fire

# ANTI-CAPITALISM

Capitalism has been challenged by forces ranging from Karl Marx to Michael Moore, some of whom have picked advertising as a sub-target.

Over the years, advertising has come under attack from feminists, socialists, anarchists, communists, anti-globalization protesters, anti-consumerists, environmentalists and anti-corporate activists. As far back as the nineteenth century, advertising was criticized for being a vulgar adjunct of commerce, by writers such as George Gissing and H. G. Wells – a critique that could be classed as 'traditionalist'.

But a more serious and widespread set of accusations has emerged from the Left – that human relationships are devalued by the process of mass consumption and mass advertising, that advertising is manipulative and promotes unnecessary purchases and waste, that it celebrates materialism, and that it assists capitalism's mania for unrestrained growth. By extension, the people who work in advertising – those who work in agencies, and the filmmakers, photographers and designers who help them put adverts together – are viewed by some anti-capitalists as conspirators engaged in the distortion of reality in pursuit of profit (although see also **No. 52, Principles**).

The activists have not effected any change in how the advertising industry actually functions, but in so far as they have changed the general climate of opinion, they have had a huge influence on advertising's output. For example, the rise of feminism in the 1970s changed the way that advertisers market to women. And the increasing awareness of environmental and ethical issues has convinced marketers to alter many products' formulation and packaging, and these changes have become the subjects of ad campaigns, such as for fair-trade coffee, cruelty-free beauty products and free-range farm produce.

In recent years, campaigners have adopted a tactic of singling out individual companies – such as Nike, McDonald's, Shell and Nestlé – for criticism of their business practices. And despite these activists' supposed antipathy to advertising, they have often created ads to convey their point. ∎

Thinner than ever.

adbusters.org

ABOVE: *Spoof ad by Adbusters, who describe themselves as 'A global network of culture jammers and creatives working to change the way information flows, the way corporations wield power, and the way meaning is produced in our society.'*

BOTTOM LEFT: No Logo, *by Naomi Klein (2000), became the textbook of the anti-globalization movement. Klein attacked brand-orientated consumer culture, and accused global corporations such as Nike of exploiting workers in the Third World.*

OPPOSITE: *Sculpture installation by Banksy, probably the most prominent critic of capitalism and advertising active today.*

NO LOGO
NAOMI KLEIN
FORLAGET

'The distortion of reality in pursuit of profit.'

# *Ads that run all over the world*

IDEA № 69

# GLOBAL ADVERTISING

The cost savings of creating a single ad to run in 100 countries are immense. But so are the challenges.

As companies began to operate internationally, they quickly saw the opportunity to achieve economies of scale by centralizing their advertising; as early as 1899, Unilever set up Lintas (Lever International Advertising Services) to create ads across multiple markets. The benefits of the strategy are clear: lower cost and consistency of messaging. But so are the pitfalls.

If a work is going to run in many countries and multiple languages, it cannot involve dialogue or wordplay, it cannot tap into local-market insights, and it cannot be tailored to local-market tastes. Some believe this means global advertising is inevitably 'dumbed down' to the level of the least sophisticated market in which it must appear. And they point to the horror shows of badly dubbed global ads that, while no doubt cheap to produce, are embarrassing to watch.

On the other hand, blockbuster commercials for the likes of Sony, Cadbury, PlayStation, Johnnie Walker and Nike are only economically feasible because they run worldwide. The ability to defray production costs across many markets also makes the fees demanded by big celebrities more affordable. And since it is very hard to come up with a great creative idea, does it not make sense for a brand to use it widely when it has one?

Some agencies also believe that – far from compromising creativity – the demands of global advertising can enhance it. That is because instead of aiming its global advertising at a lowest common denominator, an ambitious agency will search for a 'higher-order truth'. And deep human truths are not only universally relevant, they make for powerful advertising – agencies such as BBH and Wieden + Kennedy have won numerous awards for their global work. For example, BBH's global campaign for Persil/Omo ('Dirt is Good') speaks to every mother's desire to give her children freedom to play. And W+K's 'Just Do It' work for Nike is created centrally but works worldwide – since wherever there is sport, there is a will to win. ■

ABOVE: *Vodafone uses the line 'Power to you' and employs a consistent look and feel globally, but the actual concepts are created locally, as seen in this Romanian ad.*

OPPOSITE ABOVE: *Nicki Minaj in global Pepsi ad, 2012*

OPPOSITE BELOW: *Microsoft spent $100 million on this global ad campaign, through Wieden + Kennedy, 1994.*

'An ambitious agency will search for a "higher-order truth".'

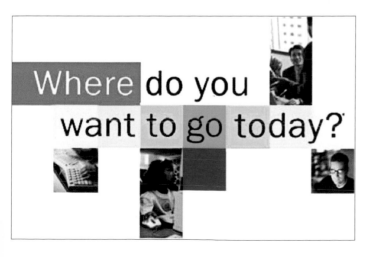

# Business-to-business advertising

## IDEA № 70
## TRADE ADS

A trade ad (also known as a business-to-business, or B2B, ad) is aimed at a company, not a consumer. Although there is a great deal of person-to-person selling in the business world, especially for high-ticket items such as tractors or passenger planes, it still helps to have a strong brand to sell.

The first trade publication was *Lloyd's List*, a shipping title founded in London in 1734. Many more were started during the great expansion of industrialization in the nineteenth century. Some trade titles are aimed at everyone in a specific industry, such as *Marketing* magazine. Others are aimed at professionals who perform a specific function within a business, such as *Purchasing* magazine, a now-defunct title that targeted purchasing agents across various industries. Today there are thousands of trade magazines around the world, and businesses are also placing huge (and increasing) volumes of B2B ads online.

The arrival of trade publications opened up a whole new market for ad agencies, and led to the formation of hundreds of new agencies specializing solely in B2B, which today accounts for almost 10 per cent of all advertising spending.

The major advantage of trade advertising is that it enables businesses to collect orders without having to go to the expense of sending a salesman. Another benefit of B2B advertising is that by making a product well known, it provides reassurance for buyers. This is important because B2B transactions are often high-risk – it does not much matter to a consumer if they buy a can of soft drink and then do not like it, but if a company spends $2 million buying industrial machinery, it is a major issue if the purchase does not work out.

And although business buyers are usually more rationally motivated than consumers, and may conduct extensive research before making a purchase, business-to-business advertising can play a role in helping the buyer justify his purchase to others in the organization, who probably have not done so much research, and who might question a decision to buy an unknown brand. No one ever got fired for buying IBM, as the saying used to go.

Some companies use consumer advertising as an indirect form of B2B marketing. Intel is a good example. It is the computer manufacturer who chooses whether to install Intel chips, not the consumer, but by making consumers feel that a computer with 'Intel Inside' is more desirable, Intel gains leverage in its negotiation with the manufacturers. ∎

TOP RIGHT: *Witty ad aimed at persuading companies to hold their conferences at the Vancouver Convention Center.*

LEFT: *Trade ads do not have to be dull, as demonstrated by this beautifully art-directed piece for Barclay's Corporate banking, by BBH London.*

OPPOSITE: *Famous ad touting the benefits of business-to-business advertising.*
© The McGraw-Hill Companies, Inc.

"I don't know who you are.

I don't know your company.

I don't know your company's product.

I don't know what your company stands for.

I don't know your company's customers.

I don't know your company's record.

I don't know your company's reputation.

Now–what was it you wanted to sell me?"

**MORAL:** Sales start **before** your salesman calls–with business publication advertising.

**McGRAW-HILL MAGAZINES**
BUSINESS•PROFESSIONAL•TECHNICAL

# Your life on screen

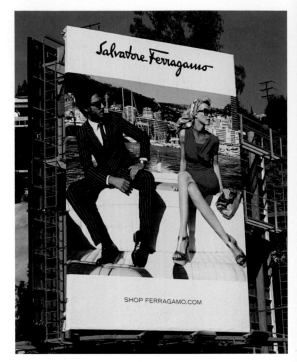

IDEA № 71

# LIFESTYLE ADVERTISING

> Most advertising focuses on communicating product benefits, but so-called lifestyle advertising, which came to prominence in the 1980s, virtually ignores the product and instead seeks to demonstrate that it understands the lifestyle of the target consumer, positioning the product as 'for people like you'.

The word 'lifestyle' was coined in 1929, by Freudian psychiatrist Alfred Adler, but there were occasional examples from the prior history of advertising that exploited the concept. An early ad for Cadillac, dating from 1903, simply used the headline 'A Summer Day and a Cadillac', saying nothing about the merits of the car, but everything about the life you might live if you owned one.

Yet the vast majority of advertising continued to be product-focused, as exemplified by the USP style championed by Rosser Reeves (see **No.38, The USP**). The only marketers who habitually talked lifestyle were those who were forbidden from addressing product attributes, as became the case with cigarette and alcohol manufacturers.

But this began to change, because society changed. The homogeneous society of the 1950s gave way to different tribes, such as the teenager, the hippy and the yuppie, making it possible to target groups by attitude. Another spur was the proliferation of brands – the average American supermarket now carries 48,750 items, according to the Food Marketing Institute – more than five times the number in 1975. So in many categories, all the potential product benefits were already 'owned', forcing new market entrants to target other areas, such as consumers' lifestyles.

The genre really took off in the 1980s. A famous example from the UK was a 1987 ad for Halifax ATMs set to the 'Easy like Sunday Morning' chorus of a track by the Commodores. The ad showed a leather-jacketed, coffee-grinding, loft-dwelling yuppie and became notorious for the emphasis it placed on depicting an aspirational lifestyle rather than a product benefit.

The argument for lifestyle advertising today is that we have reached an era where in many categories (e.g. coffee, banks, washing powder) no product has any discernible advantage over another (see **No.58, Product Parity**). But if you can produce communications that insightfully depict either the consumer's real life or the life they would like to live, then people will feel an affinity for that brand, and buy it in preference to the others. ∎

Enjoy Kopparberg responsibly

# FIND A CROWD WHO THINK
# EVERY NIGHT IS FRIDAY NIGHT
# AND YOU'LL FIND

FINDKOPPARBERG.COM

Premium
SWEDISH CIDER

149

# Consumers bombarded

IDEA № 72
# MEDIA PROLIFERATION

In 1990 there were 47 TV stations in the whole of Europe. Today there are more than 10,000. The proliferation of media, and the vast increase in the number of advertising messages that consumers are exposed to on a daily basis, is having a dramatic impact on the industry, and arguably on society.

Of course it is not just TV that has grown. The number of newspapers and magazines has exploded, and there are countless statistics on the increase in the number of websites, though Bill Clinton summed it up best: 'When I took office, only physicists had heard of what is called the World Wide Web … now even my cat has its own page.'

The key effect of media proliferation is audience fragmentation: with more TV channels, there are fewer people watching each one, so advertisers have to spend more to reach the same number of people. Today, it takes four or five airings to deliver the media weight of a single spot 20 years ago.

So the main result of media proliferation has been the proliferation of advertising. There are more ads per break on TV. Ad-filled screens are appearing in post offices, on buses and in supermarkets. Ads are being inserted into video games and iPhone apps. And out in the street, there is a race to plaster advertising on to every surface where a human eye may alight. We have gone from being exposed to about 500 ads a day back in the 1970s to around 5,000 a day today. But of course, consumers cannot absorb that much information so a huge proportion of the effort is wasted.

The smarter marketers have realized that in an era of advertising saturation, they must cut through the clutter, by being more creative, or more outrageous. Pepsi's 'Refresh' project pulled $20 million out of traditional media and re-invested it in a social entrepreneur competition. And Red Bull spent an estimated $30 million funding Felix Baumgartner's jump from the edge of space, which was watched live by 8 million viewers on YouTube. Advertisers are realizing that if they can create compelling content, they no longer need to pay to put it in front of consumers – people will seek it out themselves, online. Which proves that despite its omnipresence, consumers still do not hate advertising, they just hate bad advertising. ■

'Ad-filled screens are appearing in post offices, on buses and in supermarkets.'

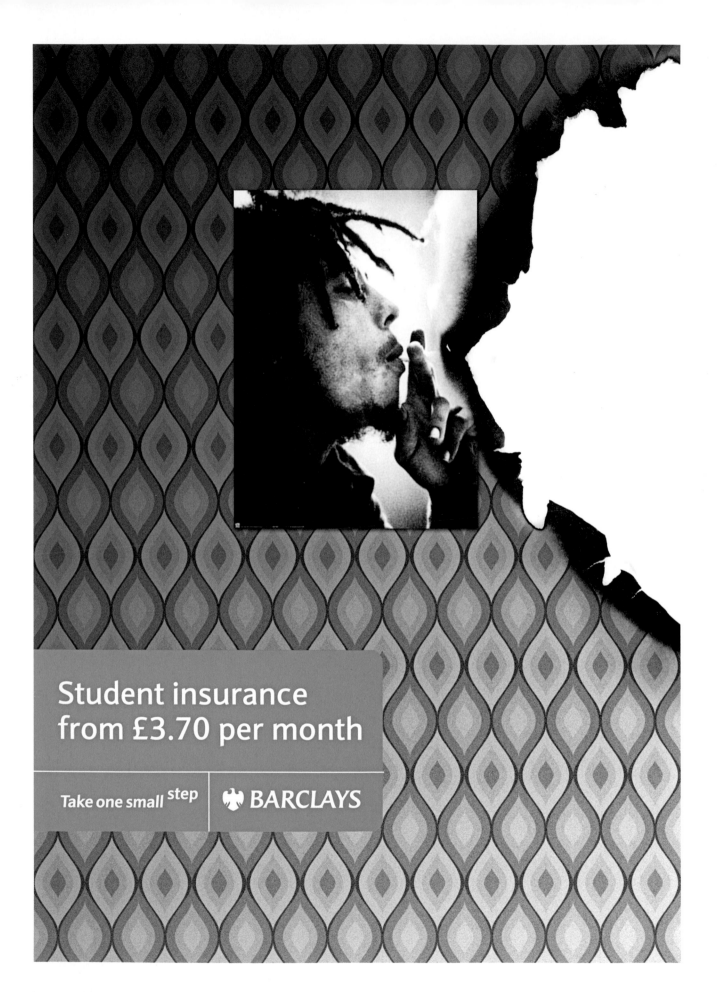

# Ads made for awards, not clients

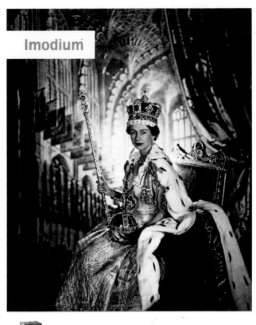

Imodium

Spending too much time on the throne?

IDEA № 73
## SCAM

Also known as 'ghost ads', scam ads are created by ad agencies purely to win awards, rather than in answer to a real brief. Sometimes the work has never run; in extreme cases the client whose logo appears on the ads is not even aware of their existence.

Scam ads are normally initiated by the agency creatives; this is understandable since they are paid and promoted on how many awards they have won. But the process is often abetted by agency managers, who are willing to risk the reputational damage of being caught since their performance is also judged partly on awards nowadays, and if their agency wins it will attract hotshot creative staff and glowing coverage in the trade press.

It is hard to say when the practice began, although it has been complained about since at least the early 1990s. The issue has exploded recently, to the point where some argue that scam is now distorting the entire industry – causing creatives to spend a disproportionate amount of time on phantom projects and some agencies to spend thousands of hours a year and millions of dollars in head-hours and productions costs creating scam ads for award shows. FP7 Doha's trophy for 2009 Agency of the Year was withdrawn by the Dubai Lynx Awards following the discovery that at least 18 of its submissions had been entered without ever being approved by the companies concerned.

But the most notorious example concerns a campaign for Kia Motors by Moma Propaganda of São Paulo, Brazil, which won two Lions at the 2011 Cannes advertising festival. The ads' paedophilic overtones subsequently caused an outrage, prompting Kia to announce that the ads had never run and were created by the agency without their knowledge. The Cannes organizers withdrew the Lions.

While the industry publicly condemns scam, many still do it, and some justify the practice (in anonymous blog comments) on the basis that awards shows ought to celebrate the best work agencies are capable of rather than just the safer ads that clients actually run. Others in the industry despise scam, and argue that an ad which has not had to go through the rigours of client approval is benefiting from an unfair advantage over ads that have – like athletes who use drugs in sporting competitions. ■

*Goodbye Kitty*

*Pet Funeral Services*
Tel: 01352 710500

# Taking on the big boys

IDEA Nº 74
# THE MICRO-NETWORK

Ad agencies started as small local businesses, then went national, and now most are part of global networks. But not every successful shop has felt the need to open offices in 100 countries – some have taken a different, and perhaps bolder, route.

A new style of agency network, pioneered by BBH and Wieden+Kennedy in the 1990s – and emulated by others, including Arnold, Mother, Fallon and Droga5 – seeks to service the entire world from a single office in each continent. The argument is that an advertiser does not need an agency in France, Spain, Portugal, etc. when a BBH or a W+K can produce all the work out of London or Portland.

For advertisers it creates a significant saving not only in ad agency fees but also their own costs, since they will require fewer marketing staff in France, Spain and Portugal. Meanwhile, the agency can charge a healthy fee because they are

working on hugely important global projects, but ideally they can staff the account with not significantly more people than would be required for a local account. And arguably, the advertiser is better off finding one really strong idea that can work across multiple markets, than developing a whole series of local ads that are each only strong enough to run in one country.

Wieden+Kennedy was founded in 1982 with Nike as its initial client and has also created renowned advertising for brands including Honda, ESPN, Microsoft and Coca-Cola. W+K is still Nike's agency of record and produces advertising for the sportswear firm in

well over 100 countries, from only nine offices (Amsterdam, Beijing, Delhi, London, New York City, Portland, São Paulo, Shanghai and Tokyo).

BBH was also founded in 1982, and has twice been Cannes Agency of the Year. From only six offices – London, New York, São Paulo, Shanghai, Singapore and Mumbai – BBH performs advertising duties for several huge brands on a worldwide basis, including Johnnie Walker, Omo/Persil and Axe/Lynx. The agency uses a network of local-market translators when adaptation of its work is required. But their ambition is to create powerful, predominantly visual advertising that can run in any market. ∎

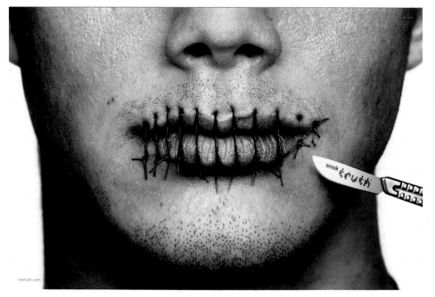

**BLACK LEVI'S.**

Levi's

**WHEN THE WORLD ZIGS, ZAG.**

*OPPOSITE: Ad for the* **'truth'** *anti-tobacco campaign, by successful micro-network Arnold Worldwide.*

*ABOVE: The first ad that BBH did for Levi's. It led to the agency adopting the black sheep as its logo.*

*RIGHT: LeBron James ad for Nike by Wieden+Kennedy, 2007.*

**WE ARE ALL WITNESSES.**

NIKEBASKETBALL.COM

# Ads without words

The rise of the visual, demonstrated by three ads for the same brand. In 1981, Lego used a visual accompanied by a headline and over 100 words of copy (right). But in later years, the copy has gradually disappeared (bottom left and opposite).

IDEA № 75
# THE RISE OF THE VISUAL

Scientific research in the 1960s began to prove that humans are primarily visual creatures and educational psychologists today estimate that 83 per cent of learning is visual. This idea filtered into advertising just at a time when art directors were beginning to play a bigger role in the creative process; the result was a revolution in what advertising looked like.

Up until the mid-twentieth century, advertising was dominated by headlines and long copy; any visuals were simply depictions of people using the product and all the creativity went into the headline. But once the notion began to take hold in the 1960s that visual ideas are more powerful, there began a significant decline in the use of headlines in ads, and a reduction in the length of copy, to the point where today, so-called long-copy ads are virtually extinct.

To some traditionalists, it is mystifying that advertising should have turned so radically against the written word, when there is plenty of evidence

that people still read. Consumers are still buying novels and newspapers. And online they are reading articles, magazines and blog posts. So why would they not read ad copy, assuming it was interesting enough? Supporters of this argument quote American adman Howard Gossage (1917–69), who famously said: 'People read what interests them, and sometimes it's an ad.'

But the world has changed since Howard Gossage's heyday. First of all, when people want more information about a product nowadays, they turn to the internet. Before that option was available, it probably made sense for the

information to be carried in a company's ads. Today, it probably does not. Secondly, people have far more entertainment choices. The commuter on the train to work, who may once have read a newspaper cover-to-cover, including the ads, can now get entertainment from an iPod, a smartphone or a handheld gaming system.

Globalization is another factor. An increasing number of marketers are centralizing their advertising activity by, for example, giving their business to a micro-network (see **No. 74, The Micro-Network**) and developing one set of ads for an entire region, or indeed the whole world. And since these 'global' ads need to work in more than one language, they tend to be visually led.

Another possible influence is the Cannes advertising awards. Because purely visual ads tend to achieve more success at Cannes – since the juries who decide on the winning ads are multinational – it may be that the rise of the visual has been accelerated by award-chasing creatives. ■

LEGO BUILDERS OF TOMORROW
1932-2007

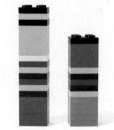

# High-tech smoke and mirrors

IDEA № 76

# DIGITAL POST-PRODUCTION

Advances in computer software have enabled advertisers to conjure the seemingly impossible; photographically realistic depictions of fantastical characters, creatures and worlds have became an everyday feature of ads in every medium.

First released in 1990, Adobe's Photoshop software transformed print advertising. Whereas image retouching was previously a laborious and limited process, with most effects needing to be achieved 'in-camera', Photoshop opened up a vast range of image-manipulation and typographical possibilities. Virtually every print ad in the world today will have been created using Photoshop.

The digital-technology revolution of the 1990s also completely revolutionized the world of TV commercials. Post-production software such as Henry, Flame and Inferno enabled visual effects that could never be achieved in real life – or at least not without enormous expense – to become standard. The move from time-consuming tape-to-tape editing to the use of software such as Avid and Final Cut Pro made editing immeasurably quicker. Digi-

tization also made sound production for radio ads unrecognizably more efficient.

And programs such as Massive, which is an artificial-intelligence-based software that duplicates people and simulates realistic crowd behaviour, have enabled advertisers to summon hordes of virtual extras to appear in their commercials. For example, PlayStation's 'Mountain' ad of 2003 featured a crowd of thousands, nearly all of them computer-generated. Two years previously, the commercial could not have been made, as the software was only created for the first *Lord of the Rings* movie, in 2001. With its perennial focus on the new, advertising has always been quick to embrace new technology.

And since advertisers have always been enamoured of exaggeration (stem-

ming perhaps from a natural desire to make dramatic claims for their products), the ability of new digital technologies to create the impossible – and to do so on a grand scale – has been embraced with open arms. Digital technology has unleashed a new wave of creativity in advertising. There are no constraints any more; if the creatives can dream it up, the computers can make it happen. ■

TOP RIGHT: *Lynx's 'Billions' commercial from 2006. It featured thousands of computer-generated women, attracted to a Lynx-spraying man on a beach.*

LEFT: *Dove's 2006 'Evolution' spot – part of the brand's 'Campaign For Real Beauty' – highlighted the inhuman level of perfection that Photoshop has accustomed us to.*

OPPOSITE: *Evian's 2009 'Rollerskating Babies' commercial is a perfect example of the kind of creativity made possible by new technology.*

'Virtually every print ad in the world today will have been created using Photoshop.'

# Hitting them with irony

BOTTOM LEFT: *Explicitly postmodern campaign for UK insurer esure, in which Michael Winner urged a flustered woman: 'Calm down, dear – it's only a commercial.'*

OPPOSITE TOP: *UK insurance comparison website Go Compare, responding to the public's dislike of their opera-singing spokesman, took the postmodern step of graffiti-ing their own poster sites, 2012.*

OPPOSITE BOTTOM: *Carlton Draught's 'Big Ad' – the ultimate parody?*

IDEA № 77

# POSTMODERNISM

Hundreds of books have been written about postmodernism – most of them densely complex, and in French. But for advertising, a simple definition is that it involves the use of *irony* as a selling-tool.

Irony itself can be elusive to define, but in ads it usually means the ridiculing of conventional persuasive techniques. As far back as 1932, Jack Benny told this joke about the sponsor of his radio show: 'I was driving across the Sahara Desert when I came across a party of people who had been stranded for 30 days without a drop of water, and they were ready to perish. I gave each of them a glass of Canada Dry Ginger Ale, and not one of them said it was a bad drink.'

But for centuries advertising was dominated by 'straight' messages, often presented by a voice of authority, and aiming for credibility; only in the mid-1990s was there a burgeoning of ads with what might be called an 'ironic selling proposition', which deliberately undermined their own credibility – perhaps the credibility of advertising itself – for the purposes of entertainment.

In 2005, Australian beer Carlton Draught produced possibly the most ironically self-aware commercial of all time. Known as 'The Big Ad', the commercial parodied advertising epics such as the British Airways 'Face' ad from the 1980s. To the soundtrack of Carl Orff's *Carmina Burana*, thousands of robed men sang lyrics including: 'It's a big ad we're in! My God it's big! It's just so freaking huge! Expensive ad! This ad better sell some bloody beer!'

Some within the industry condemn ironic advertising for being self-referential. But in its quest to appeal to mass audiences, advertising has always tapped into shared knowledge – hence there are many ads that reference well-known films or TV shows. Now that advertising has itself become a mass-culture phenomenon, it is perhaps not surprising to see advertising that echoes other advertising. ■

'The use of irony as a selling tool.'

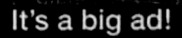

It's a big ad!

# A meeting before the meeting

IDEA Nº 78
# THE TISSUE MEETING

In a 'tissue meeting' a variety of different creative routes are shared with the client as ideas in progress, rather than a more formal presentation of just one solution. And depending on who you listen to, it is either the best or the worst change in the history of how ad agencies operate.

The name derives from the thin pieces of paper that an agency uses for presenting early-stage concepts, as opposed to the stiff polyboard used for fully worked-up ideas, and the technique was invented in the late 1980s by HHCL in the UK and Chiat\Day in the US. They believed that discussing their thinking early on would encourage clients to take shared ownership of ideas, and that a collaborative process would produce better results than if the agency went away and worked in isolation before returning to unveil its solution with a grand 'ta-da'. An interim check-in meeting can also help ensure the agency is not wasting its time with work that is completely off-brief (when a project goes back to the drawing-board, it is very costly for the agency).

But the most important goal was to encourage clients to buy braver advertising. Steve Henry and Jay Chiat felt that showing a wider range of creative ideas would give them licence to push the boundaries of the brief, whereas if only one idea was shown (which was how nearly all agencies operated at the time) there would always be pressure to make it just what the client had ordered, rather than something truly mould-breaking. The strategy certainly worked for both HHCL and Chiat\Day, who became known for irreverent and iconoclastic work.

Today, the tissue meeting has become an extremely widespread industry practice. But not everyone approves. Some in the advertising business feel that it is hard enough coming up with *one* good idea for a campaign, so the requirement to present multiple routes not only dilutes the agency's efforts, it creates a risk that the client will choose something mediocre. John Hegarty, a founding partner of Bartle Bogle Hegarty, writes in *Hegarty on Advertising* that 'whoever came up with the completely stupid idea of tissue meetings should be taken outside and shot'. ∎

YOU KNOW WHEN YOU'VE BEEN TANGO'D

IDEA № 79
# AMBIENT

'Ambient' can mean ads that appear anywhere from outer space to students' foreheads – anywhere, that is, except in the conventional media. At its best, the use of ambient media can create powerful, provocative ads.

It came to the fore in the 1990s, as an attempt to break through the ever-increasing advertising clutter that consumers are exposed to in the traditional media. Examples have included messages on parking tickets, coffee cups, the pavement, apples, supermarket trolleys, zeppelins and ashtrays. It also includes techniques such as projecting films or images on to buildings, and we are now seeing the emergence of 'digital ambient' – for example, digital panels that consumers can send texts to with their mobiles, or augmented-reality (AR) executions.

The great advantage of ambient advertising is that because it appears in an unexpected place, it can surprise consumers, and 'cut through'. And because the execution can be so perfectly tailored to where it is placed – e.g. anti-drink driving ads at the bottom of a beer glass – the brand message can be delivered in a highly relevant way. There is also something exciting about the fact that ambient ads are real – not just a picture of a thing, like on TV or a print ad, but the actual thing itself.

Critics of the form point out that ambient ads – especially the one-off, site-specific executions – tend not to be seen by as many people as conventional media and therefore are not worth the money. The counter argument is that a highly creative ambient ad generates PR, and if it is featured in a national or big-city newspaper, will reach many millions of people.

Although ambient advertising is often stunty, irreverent and sometimes not even approved by the local council (known as 'guerrilla' advertising), even big brands may dabble in it, hoping to appear fun and nimble, or to bring an otherwise passive campaign right up into consumers' faces. But since the effectiveness of ambient is not easily measurable, marketers are wary of committing significant funds to it. For that reason, ambient executions are sometimes funded by the ad agency themselves, having been proactively conceived by the creatives as a means to get interesting work produced, or for the purposes of entering awards. ∎

RIGHT: *This sculpture of a Volkswagen Polo made out of ice promoted a deal where the car came with free air-conditioning.*

BELOW: *Fun ambient piece for McDonalds, by TBWA Switzerland.*

OPPOSITE: *Ambient execution by JWT London – a nice addition to the long-running KitKat campaign.*

'Even big brands may dabble in it, hoping to appear fun and nimble.'

# The pocket communicator

IDEA № 80
## MOBILE

There are now more mobile devices than people on the planet. And five times more people own a mobile than a PC. We also care about them a lot; we take them with us everywhere we go – even sleep next to them at night. The potential of mobile as an advertising medium is huge.

The first portable handset was invented in 1973, mobile phones entered the mass market in the early 1990s, and the first mobile phone advertising appeared in the year 2000 when a Finnish news provider offered free news headlines via text message (SMS), sponsored by advertising. SMS advertising is still extremely popular, with some justification, since few other ads land straight in the hands of the potential customer. The redemption of coupons sent via SMS is notably higher than the rate for coupons printed in newspapers.

But it was the introduction of the smartphone that really opened up the possibilities for mobile advertising. The first big hit came in 2008 and was for UK brewer Carling; their iPint app, which allows users to pretend they are drinking beer from their phone, has been downloaded over 3 million times. Making use of the iPhone's built-in accelerometer technology, it was an execution that simply would not have been possible in any other medium.

A 2008 mobile campaign by the Admob agency for Land Rover North America demonstrated the power of mobile as a sales tool. During the campaign period, 73 per cent of traffic to Land Rover's mobile website came as a result of users clicking through from these ads. The campaign generated 45,000 video views, 5,000 dealer look-ups, 800 brochure requests and 1,100 click-to-calls – another feature that only mobile can offer.

There are now over 2.2 billion smartphones in use worldwide, with a wealth of possibilities for advertisers – clickable banners at the top or bottom of the screen, mobile video ads, advertising within mobile games, interstitials that appear while a mobile web page is loading, not to mention even more advanced features such as apps, QR codes and augmented reality. Although still in its infancy, and with only 1 per cent of total advertising expenditure, it is highly possible that mobile is the future of advertising. ∎

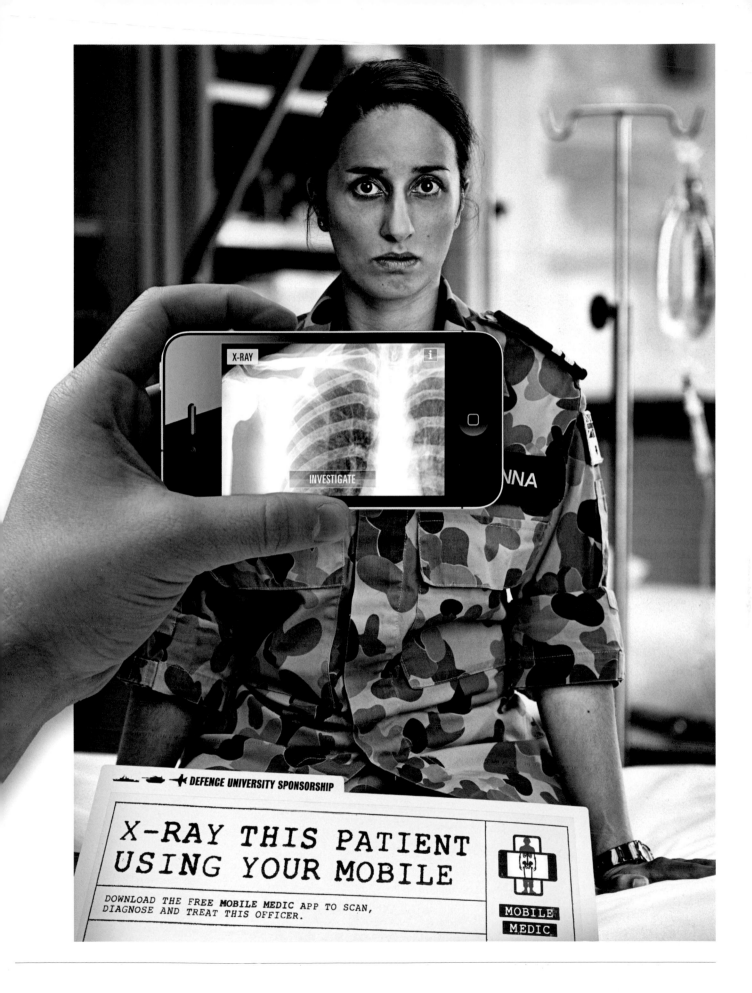

*Paying attention to retention*

# CUSTOMER-RELATIONSHIP MARKETING

Companies spend millions on advertising to attract new customers. But what about the ones they already have? The insight that it is easier – and cheaper – to retain an existing customer than attract a new one has created an entire sub-industry within advertising known as customer-relationship marketing (CRM).

CRM can involve communicating with a company's existing customers in order to nurture and retain them, targeting prospective customers, or persuading former clients back into the fold. It grew out of 1980s database marketing, whose 'personalized' letters went to countless customers. Today's more sophisticated CRM practices allow a company to send information only to the right people at the right time, thus saving a huge amount of money compared to mass mailings, the majority of which end up in the recycling bin.

The normal method of communication is direct mail (DM) or, increasingly, EDM (electronic direct mail), which is even cheaper and offers the additional advantage that the company can track exactly who read it, who deleted it and who acted on it.

This measurability is attractive to marketers. For example, in 2009, direct-marketing agency LIDA targeted existing Mini owners with a series of communications that reflected the car's fun personality. One email linked to a game called Mini Roulette, which averaged 3.4 goes per visitor, for almost two minutes each. For £100,000, it helped sell almost £23 million worth of Minis – a return on investment of £245 for every £1 spent.

But CRM is not just used for selling – it can also play a role in relationship-building. First Choice holidays noticed there is a huge gap between when people book their trip and when they depart, and decided to contact customers during that intervening period, providing them with a tailored post-booking experience, with information ranging from minutiae such as airport parking, to exploring what they could do on holiday. Login rates were over 62 per cent, and 90 per cent of customers agreed that the company 'really brought my holiday to life', no doubt considerably increasing the odds that the customer would book their next holiday through First Choice. ∎

*LEFT: First Choice. The holiday company has been a CRM pioneer.*

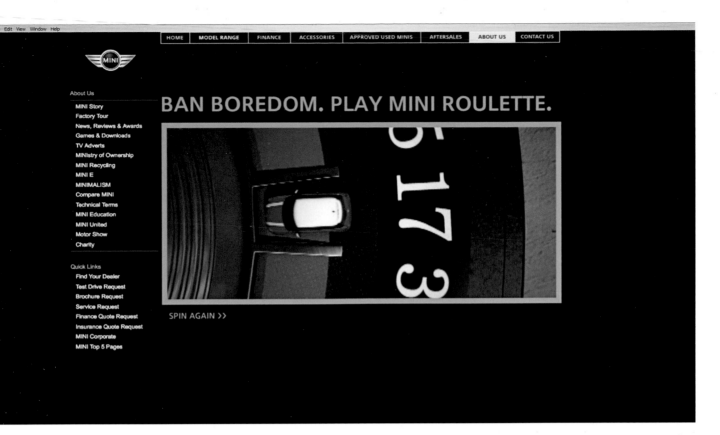

'For less than £100,000, it helped sell almost £23 million worth of Minis.'

*ABOVE: Mini Roulette, by LIDA.*

*RIGHT: Existing Procter & Gamble customers were sent an email introducing them to the 'Flash Hunk' promotional site, where they were rewarded with a cheeky Chippendale demonstrating cleaning products and the chance to win £10,000.*

BOTTOM LEFT: *A Cannes Grand Prix winner in 2011, this campaign by Droga5 New York was a media tour de force. Over 300 pages of Jay-Z's autobiography were placed out in the world, including on the bottom of the Delano Hotel's pool in Miami. The locations were searchable via campaign sponsor Bing.*

OPPOSITE TOP: *Creative and media working hand in hand: this UK poster for Google Voice Search employing a phonetic spelling of 'Piccadilly Circus' appeared on a poster site at ... Piccadilly Circus.*

OPPOSITE BOTTOM: *In 2010, British yogurt company Yeo Valley negotiated directly with ITV to buy spots for its 'rapping farmers' ad in the X Factor – completely bypassing their media agency.*

IDEA № 82
# SEPARATION OF MEDIA

From the 1840s, nearly all agencies were 'full service' – they both created the advertising and bought the media it was placed in. But when holding companies such as WPP and Omnicom began to acquire multiple ad agencies, they hived off the media departments into larger stand-alone entities, for greater buying power.

In 1989, Saatchi & Saatchi spun off its various media planning and buying functions into a separate company called Zenith and, in 1999, WPP Group created Mindshare from the media departments of Ogilvy & Mather and J. Walter Thompson. By the year 2000, there were hardly any agencies left who bought their own media.

The rationale was simple: a larger media specialist could use its weight to buy media more cheaply. But the unbundling also meant that media executives, who had previously been the backroom boys whose media recommendations were relegated to the last five minutes of a creative presentation, now received their fair share of the limelight. Today, with the increasing fragmentation and complexity of media, this formerly unsexy part of the industry is thriving.

However, a criticism of ad agencies that are no longer full service is that their ideas are often developed with an insufficient understanding of the media possibilities. And most media agencies have never seen the advertising material when they start work on the media plan – which must surely hamper their ability to deliver an integrated and insightful solution (see **No. 91, Media Neutrality**).

Some creative agencies therefore have begun to re-add media capabilities to their offering, at least in terms of media planning – buying remains external. At the same time, many media agencies are starting to offer creative services in-house. But it is also possible that instead of this 're-bundling', a further split may take place, with the media agencies themselves splitting into two, between those involved in the more innovative planning functions, and the media buyers, whose world is becoming increasingly technology-driven and automated. ∎

'By the year 2000, there were hardly any agencies left who bought their own media.'

# Offices without offices

IDEA № 83

# OPEN PLAN

The elimination of individual offices and the placing of staff in an open-plan environment, which started to take hold in the 1990s, has been the single biggest change in the physical layout of advertising agencies. Its effects are hotly debated.

Open plan certainly costs less per capita, since the lack of walls makes it a more efficient use of space. Plus it has the advantage of flexibility – it is easier to move people and teams around when no walls need to be knocked down. But the real benefit is held to be that open plan creates a more collaborative working environment. It is certainly undeniable that an open-plan office generates more 'buzz'. Visitors to ad agency creative departments in the days before open plan were invariably surprised to find that a place they had expected to be a pulsating hive of activity had more of the feel of a library, or a morgue.

But the peace and quiet served a purpose. Although certain teams within an agency, such as the account handlers, thrive on the energy and interaction of open plan, the creatives can struggle with the distractions it brings: for many, noise and interruptions destroy the 'flow state' they find most productive for thinking up ideas.

The detractors of open plan can also point to research that links it with higher levels of stress, conflict and staff turnover – and lower levels of productivity. Surveys also consistently show that, given the choice, employees prefer closed offices. It is also somewhat ironic that the senior agency managers who have implemented these open-plan arrangements do not normally give up their own offices (although admittedly, higher-ranking staff could be said to require a private space since a part of their job involves discussing confidential matters).

Most agencies today have reached a compromise; they place their staff in an open-plan setting, but also provide them with access, when required, to a quiet workspace. ■

LEFT: *JWT Paris. The cutting-edge design is entirely open plan, but glass-doored 'caves' are provided as meeting rooms.*

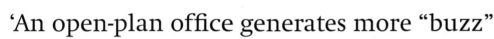

'An open-plan office generates more "buzz".'

'Early virals ... used shock tactics
to gain attention.'

*Viral campaign for Trojan condoms,
by the Viral Factory, which parodied
Olympic events – substituting them
with sexual 'sports' such as 'Pelvic
Power Lifting'.*

# Infectiously entertaining

IDEA № 84
# VIRAL MARKETING

When someone shares an ad with a friend, the advertising idea is passed from one to the other – like an infection. And if each infected person goes on to infect two more, then the virus spreads exponentially, and a film can receive millions of views in a few hours.

*ABOVE: This successful video for Nike, featuring Brazilian footballer Ronaldinho repeatedly hitting the crossbar, capitalized on one of the internet's favourite debates– 'real or fake?'*

*BELOW: One of the most popular viral videos of all time, Pepsi's 'Gladiator' ad of 2004 has racked up 47 million views.*

The phenomenon of the viral ad emerged as soon as people were able to forward online videos to their friends in the mid-1990s. And the term 'viral marketing' – usually referring to web videos, but which could actually be anything shareable, like a text message, a game or an email – was first popularized in a 1996 article in *Fast Company* magazine entitled 'The Virus of Marketing'.

Early virals exploited the more lax regulation of web films compared to TV advertising and used shock tactics to gain attention, or adopted a 'too sexy for TV' approach. Some caused outrage – for example, a 2003 viral film for Ford that featured a cat being decapitated had to be disowned by both the advertising agency responsible and the car company, who both claimed they had not approved it.

Virals have always had a slightly racy reputation, but for sound reasons not many people would forward a corporate sales pitch to a friend; to go viral successfully, an ad has to be very rude, shocking, bizarre or amazing. Many use a mockumentary film technique, or computer-animated sleight of hand, prompting viewers to wonder 'How did they do that?' or 'Is this real?'

The game-changing advantage of a viral film is that advertisers are able to get consumers to view their commercials without having to pay for TV airtime, although many viral campaigns are in fact launched with a paid-for 'seeding strategy', which acts as an accelerant. This can include placement of the film on high-traffic websites, or targeting of socially connected individuals, such as people who run popular blogs, who can feed it out to their readers. But the hope is that the film then spreads by itself. (See also **No. 95, Facebook**.) ∎

# Joining the conversation

IDEA Nº 85
## SOCIAL MEDIA

There are almost as many definitions of social media as there are social-media websites, but in short, social media refers to the methods that people use to share things on the internet. And its development has had huge implications for the advertising industry.

First of all, the sheer amount of time people are spending on social media sites makes it impossible for marketers to ignore (the average Facebook user, for example, spends seven hours a month on the site) – and hundreds of new 'social media agencies' have sprung up to help advertisers capitalize on the new medium. But more importantly, social media has initiated a seismic shift in the way advertisers communicate with consumers. (See also **No. 95, Facebook**.)

Before social media, advertising was purely a monologue – marketers 'transmitted' their messages to consumers, via what might be termed the 'traditional' media, such as newspapers and television. But social media is understood as more conversational, which means that, via blogs or social-networking pages, brands can enter into a dialogue with consumers.

Although traditional media offers the advantage of control (a TV ad can be carefully crafted, whereas a conversation on social media cannot) it is expensive. Social media, on the other hand, is free, or almost free (for example, it may involve the minimal cost of sending product samples to prominent bloggers).

But not only is social media an effective way for brands to communicate with people, it can also be a valuable source of consumer intelligence. Since the cars people drive or the places where they buy their coffee do play a role in their lives, many online conversations naturally touch on brands. The vast majority of marketers (74 per cent, as of August 2011) have therefore begun to employ social-media monitoring – gathering a wealth of information on what people think about their products, from what they are saying about them on blogs, forums, Twitter, etc. This data can deliver insights that then help to create new ad campaigns – even new products. ∎

In 2010, agency W+K created a social media masterstroke: 120 videos in 24 hours featuring the 'Old Spice guy', who delivered personal video responses – sometimes within minutes – to comments posted on Twitter, Facebook and YouTube.

## *The fastest-growing medium ever*

IDEA № 86
# ONLINE ADVERTISING

Online advertising started as a tiny market, offering simple static display ads that mimicked the form of print ads. Today it is not just the most creatively dynamic medium in the industry, it has become the second-biggest medium after television. And the gap is narrowing.

Unlike newspaper or magazine ads, online ads can be transmitted instantly to anywhere on the planet, so distribution costs are close to zero, and production costs are also much lower, since the ads do not have to be printed. But although an early US online service provider called Prodigy carried ads in the 1980s, they were graphically unsophisticated, and revenues did not take off.

The breakthrough came with the invention of clickable banner ads in 1994. Click-throughs are easily measured, meaning the ROI (return on investment) of an online ad is much easier to determine than for a print campaign. And since individual executions in a campaign can be measured separately, it is a simple task for marketers to determine which of their ads are working and which are not. The earliest banner ads had click-through rates (CTR) as high as 50 per cent, although today, a typical CTR is less than 0.2 per cent.

The next advance came in 1995 with the release of the first ad server, which stored adverts centrally and delivered them automatically to website visitors, creating huge economies of scale. Innovation has continued apace in online advertising, with the introduction of Google AdWords to deliver contextually relevant ads, social media campaigns on Facebook and Twitter, homepage take-overs and video ads.

But online advertising has its critics, who complain about threats to privacy (companies tracking your browsing histories in order to serve more relevant ads), slow loading times (many ads use Flash-based graphics, which delay the loading of a website) and spyware (ads that, when clicked on, alter a user's homepage, or spawn pop-ups). Some internet users have begun installing browser plug-ins such as AdBlock to eliminate advertising from their web experience. Nevertheless, online ad spend has grown exponentially, and with annual US revenue of $39.5 billion, it overtook print advertising in 2012. ∎

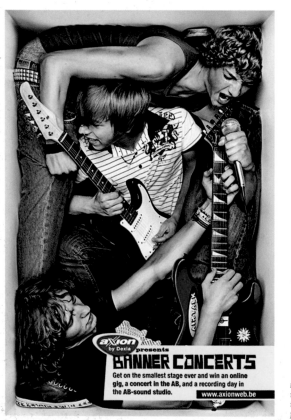

LEFT: *Axion bank, whose target market is young people, launched an innovative series of concerts that took place within banner ads.*

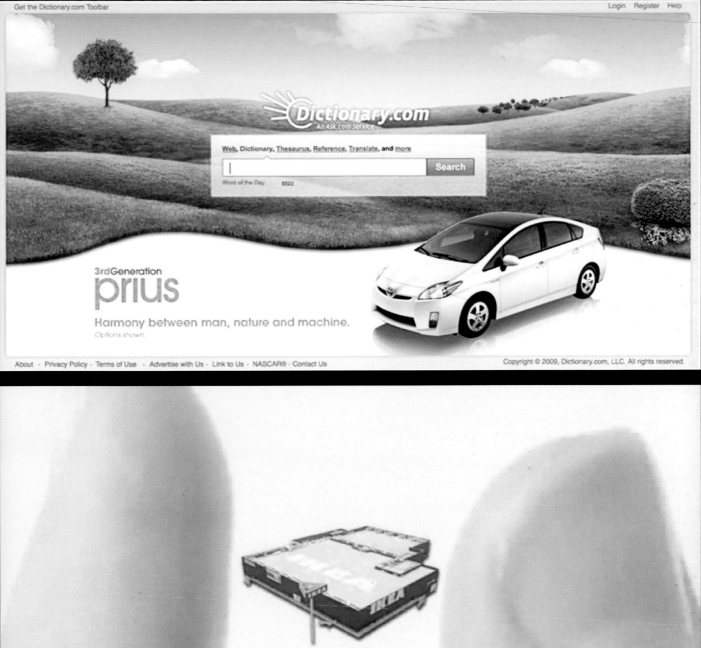

*TOP: Beautifully clean takeover of
the Dictionary.com homepage for
Toyota Prius.*

'Distribution costs are close to zero.'

*End of the percentage game*

BELOW: *Coca-Cola is one of many clients now introducing a PBR (payment by results) component into their remuneration plan – which means the ad agency earns more if its ads work ... and less if they do not.*

IDEA № 87

# DECLINE OF THE COMMISSION SYSTEM

Ad agencies were initially paid via a commission on the media they booked for clients. But gradually, this was replaced with a fee payment system – and when you change how someone is paid, you change how they behave.

Under the commission system, agencies actually did not charge their clients anything at all, but earned a discount (typically 15 per cent) from media owners, such as newspapers and TV stations. So if a marketer gave an agency $1 million to buy media for a campaign, the agency paid $850,000 for it (because of the 15 per cent discount) and kept the remaining $150,000 as its income.

But in the late 1950s, as TV advertising costs rose substantially, and thus agency remuneration did too, clients felt their agencies were overpaid. In response, the American Association of National Advertisers (ANA) proposed simply paying agencies a fee for their services, rather than a commission on media booked. Agencies stubbornly resisted the move, and it only became widespread after the split into 'media' and 'creative' shops in the 1990s (see **No.82, Separation of Media**), after which the creative agencies were no longer responsible for booking media so in fact *could not* be paid via commission.

Although the change generally led to agencies earning less, it also had a more subtle but far-reaching effect on their *mindset*. Under the commission system, agencies had an incentive to get their work on air. If no ad ran, they were not paid. But under the fee system, an agency is paid according to how many hours its staff work on the client's business, so it could be argued that it has an incentive to spin the process out, a criticism levelled at other 'pay by the hour' professions such as lawyers and management consultants.

On the other hand, the change helped to free agencies from bias. Whereas before they had an incentive to recommend the most expensive media possible (i.e. television), today an agency is free to recommend whatever it feels will be most effective, since its remuneration is not connected to the media spend. ∎

180

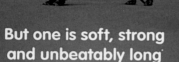

**Some are long**

**But one is soft, strong and unbeatably long**

Andrex White

**Spend your pennies wisely**
*excluding longer lasting/double roll products

LEFT: *Paying an agency simply for the time spent on creating an idea is arguably inadequate compensation for powerful campaigns such as the 'Andrex Puppy', which began in 1972 and is still running today.*

BELOW: *In 1960, Shell caused shockwaves when it became the first major advertiser to pay its ad agency (at the time, Ogilvy) on a fee, rather than commission, basis.*

'It also had a more subtle but far-reaching effect on their mindset.'

SHELL

**FILL UP – and feel the difference**

# Party time in ad-land

IDEA № 88

## THE DOT-COM BOOM

In the late 1990s, investors pumped fortunes into seemingly any company with a '.com' in its name. Lacking a bricks-and-mortar presence, these firms splashed out heavily on advertising to create awareness: at the peak of the tech bubble, dot-com firms were spending $1.09 on marketing for every $1 of revenue, causing an unprecedented boom in the ad industry.

With hindsight, it looks like madness, but at the time, these companies believed there would only be room for one online player in each category, and they were in a 'race for fame': Super Bowl XXXIV in January 2000 featured 17 dot-com companies, who each paid over $2 million for a 30-second spot.

But when the NASDAQ crashed in April 2000, many of the tech-stocks failed. By the time of the next Super Bowl in 2001, the number of dot-com firms advertising had shrunk to three. There followed hundreds of lay-offs in the ad industry as the dot-coms turned into dot-bombs.

The bust was certainly not due to poor advertising – in fact many dot-com commercials were of excellent quality. A 1998 Super Bowl ad for online electrical retailer Outpost.com – by agency Cliff Freeman & Partners – which featured attempts to fire gerbils through the 'o' of the company's logo, won over a dozen advertising awards, including a Grand Clio. But although in 2000 Outpost. com's stock price reached $60 per share, one year later the company was sold to a competitor for just 25 cents a share.

Online fashion retailer Boo.com launched in autumn 1999 with another acclaimed campaign, but the idea was ahead of its time, the execution faulty and, having burned through $135 million of venture capital in just 18 months – much of it spent on advertising – the company went bankrupt in May 2000.

Pets.com created a wildly popular sock puppet advertising mascot, via TBWA\Chiat\Day San Francisco. The puppet made appearances on ABC's *Good Morning America*, *Nightline* and *Live with Regis and Kathie Lee*; it even featured as a balloon in the 1999 Macy's Thanksgiving Day Parade. In January 2000 the company launched a Super Bowl ad, reputedly costing $1.2 million, the witty tagline of which explained why the world needed an online pet store: 'Because pets can't drive!' But the company's finance department was not as skilled as its marketing department; Pets.com closed in November 2000, having consumed $300 million of investment capital.

Gradually, the internet economy found its feet, and many online-only companies have returned to mainstream advertising, but at a more sensible pace. Advertisers in the 2013 Super Bowl included GoDaddy, ETrade and Cars.com. ∎

*Print ad for Boo.com, by BMP DDB*
*London, 1999.*

'The penetration of DVRs in US households has now reached almost 50 per cent.'

# The ad zapper

## IDEA № 89
# TIVO

In 1999, TiVo introduced a digital video recorder (DVR) that some feared would be a catastrophe for advertising, since it allowed consumers to skip through commercials at 32x speed. Other models even had technology that removed the commercials entirely.

Although consumers had been able to fast-forward ads since the advent of video cassette recorders (VCR) in the 1970s, VCRs were notoriously tricky to program, and in fact only 22 per cent of owners regularly used them to record TV shows; most shows were still watched 'live', so their ads were not being skipped. But hard-disk-based DVRs made recording of TV programmes much easier – consumers could record a whole TV series with just one press of a button. TiVo grew so popular that the verb 'to TiVo' became the generic term in the US for 'to record on a DVR'. The penetration of DVRs in US households has now reached almost 50 per cent. Within those homes, a huge proportion of the ads during time-shifted viewing – estimates range from 65 to 85 per cent – are being zapped.

The threat to the TV advertising business is clear. TiVo and its competitors have faced several lawsuits from media companies, and the government of Singapore has gone as far as banning TiVo, in an attempt to protect its media industry.

In response to the rise of the DVR, marketers are beginning to change how they advertise their products on TV. Product placement and branded content are growing rapidly, since a commercial message cannot be skipped if it is integrated into the programme (see **No. 14, Product Placement**). There has also been an increase in 'banners' – ad overlays along the bottom of the screen.

But mass DVR ownership is in its infancy, and its effects are as yet unclear. It is worth pointing out that total time-shifted viewing in DVR households is still only around 14 per cent: it seems that not everyone wants to schedule their viewing – most just want to sit back and have it wash over them. It may also be that advertising's fears of Armageddon are partly based on poor maths: if 50 per cent of households have DVRs, and 14 per cent of their TV consumption is time-shifted, within which 65 per cent of the ads are fast-forwarded, then only 50 x 14 x 65 per cent = 4.5 per cent of total ad impressions are being avoided. ■

TOP: *In 2013, British supermarket Sainsbury's launched a TV show called 'What's Cooking?' on Channel 4. One advantage of 'branded content' is that the commercial message is integrated with the content, whereas commercials in ad breaks can be skipped by DVRs.*

ABOVE: *Ads known as 'banners', 'bugs', and 'snipes' are increasingly appearing on-screen during the programmes.*

OPPOSITE: *Product placement in TV shows avoids the problem of ad-skipping.*

BOTTOM LEFT: *Contextual advertising placement is performed automatically by computer software ... occasionally leading to unintended consequences.*

# *Ads that know what you are looking for*

IDEA № 90
# SEARCH

It would be very difficult to overstate the impact Google has had on advertising. Having completely decimated the classified ad business in newspapers, Google dominates a giant new sub-category of the ad industry – 'search advertising', which now accounts for half of all online adspend.

The first search ad was created by Yahoo! in 1996, which placed targeted banners when users searched for the keyword 'golf'. Keywords are the basis of all search advertising. Google's AdWords software, which it introduced in 2000, reads what you type into the Google search box and serves up ads for related businesses. These businesses bid – in real-time auctions – to have their ad triggered when you type certain keywords.

At first, search advertising was sold on the basis of cost per thousand views, which followed the model of the newspaper industry, but in 2003 Google began to offer pay per click (PPC), under which advertisers only pay when a user clicks on their ad.

Since consumers often use Google to research purchasing options, or find a business that can supply a service for them, the ability of search advertising to target consumers with a tailored ad at exactly the time they are looking to buy, and then to allow them to click directly through to the company's website, is highly attractive to advertisers. The most valuable search keywords are those typed in by a user who appears to be interested in making an expensive purchase, such as a holiday or a home loan.

A whole new class of advertising agencies specializing in search-engine marketing has arisen to help businesses make the most of Google AdWords. And search engine optimization, or SEO, has become an important battleground for advertisers. The goal of SEO is to ensure a company appears as high as possible in search results. Techniques include making sure that a website consistently uses the actual phrases that people type into search boxes, optimizing the site's source code, and working with the search-engine companies to make sure that the site is easily accessible to them. Successful SEO is essential, since the average click-through rate for page 1 of Google's search results is 8.9 per cent, but it drops to 1.5 per cent for sites on page 2. ∎

186

*RIGHT: A Google search for 'business cards' triggers adverts for companies that offer this service, both at the top of the search results, and in a column to the side.*

*BELOW: German car rental firm Sixt used these fun ASCII-character executions for its Google ads – and received 47 per cent more visitors than usual.*

'Search engine optimization ... has become an important battleground for advertisers.'

# The struggle against media bias

IDEA № 91
## MEDIA NEUTRALITY

Many ad agencies are specialized – they focus solely on social media, direct advertising or above-the-line. But a new breed of agency rejects that model, claiming it results in biased thinking. As a quote on Naked's website explains: 'If you ask a butcher what to have for dinner, he's probably not going to recommend salad.'

For most of the history of advertising, most agencies were 'full service' – they both created the ads and booked the media. But from the mid-1990s they began to split into separate creative and media agencies (see **No. 82, Separation of Media**). At the same time, an explosion of new media channels led to the formation of a further raft of specialist agencies to handle digital, sales promotion, social media, etc.

Although the move towards specialization meant that advertisers could access expert knowledge in each discipline, the issue it created was that if a marketer went to a digital agency they would only be offered a digital solution to their problem, and if they went to a sales-promotion agency, they would only be offered sales-promotion ideas – it seemed no one could offer them a bird's eye view of their overall communications needs.

And even if the marketer was able to figure out for themselves that their optimal media buy was, say, a TV commercial and a Facebook app, or a print campaign and a series of web banners, there was no single agency that could deliver a big idea that worked across all of these media, since none of the specialist agencies had an incentive to come up with an idea bigger than their individual discipline. As Sir Martin Sorrell put it: 'If you make money playing the piano, there's little incentive to compose for an orchestra.'

Change came in 2000, when Naked Communications developed a philosophy they called 'media neutrality', which meant a willingness (and ability) to offer clients the best solution to meet their communication needs, whatever the medium. Today, the advertising landscape is mixed. A few agencies have followed the Naked model, but most are still highly specialized, although they may claim that they can offer the full range of disciplines via partner agencies. For example, nearly all of Sorrell's WPP agencies are specialists, but they offer clients access to other disciplines via other companies in the WPP group. ∎

FELIX
BAUMGARTNER

WORLD ACTION SPORTSPERSON
OF THE YEAR

# Branded games

IDEA № 92

# ADVERGAMES

From the days of Atari and Pong, when it was a niche hobby, gaming has exploded to the point where the vast majority of the US population now plays video games (83 per cent, according to a 2009 study by TNS Global). Advertisers could not ignore the pastime's popularity and began creating their own branded games.

The earliest, from companies such as General Mills, Coca-Cola and Samsung, date from around 1995 and were created on floppy disk, which made them difficult to distribute since advertisers had to put them physically into the hands of consumers. Reebok had some success giving away CD-ROM games in a basketball magazine (1998) and in its shoeboxes (1999).

But it was the growth of the internet as a gaming platform that saw advergaming take off, and numerous companies nowadays provide some sort of game on their website, or release branded games to the popular 'casual gaming' sites. The purpose of these games is usually just to provide the consumer with entertainment, while making the advertiser seem fun and relevant. The games are often 're-skinned' versions of arcade classics, and the branding is delivered by featuring a company's products as power-ups, or items to be collected.

In 2006, Crispin Porter + Bogusky created three Xbox games for Burger King, which all featured the company's 'King' character. Not only did they provide Burger King's target audience of young men with a fun branded experience, they actually generated revenues for the burger chain – 2.7 million copies of the games were sold instore, at $3.99 each.

Some games have more of an educational aspect. For example, the ability of a video game to simulate the challenges of military operations have made advergaming a natural approach for the world's armed forces. The US, UK and New Zealand militaries are among several to have used games as a recruitment tool.

Rather than going to the expense of creating their own games, another way advertisers can reach the gaming audience is to buy advertising space within commercially released video or computer games – a format known as in-game advertising. Players seem to have little problem with this potentially intrusive form of advertising since, for example in a driving game, the placement of adverts around a track actually adds to the realism, mimicking the signage found at real-world racing circuits. ∎

'Making the advertiser seem fun and relevant.'

# Shows that are really ads

OPPOSITE: 'Who is Johnny X?', an award-winning series of nine online films for the Sony Ericsson X1 phone, 2008.

BELOW: 'Dumb Ways To Die' was a supremely catchy public-safety message produced by McCann Melbourne for Metro Trains in 2012. The three-minute film has been viewed over 68 million times on YouTube.

BOTTOM: 'McDonalds Gets Grilled' aired on Channel 7 in Australia in 2012. The documentary was funded by the fast-food giant and aimed to give consumers an honest and transparent picture of its food preparation methods.

IDEA № 93

# BRANDED CONTENT

Companies had been sponsoring programmes since the early days of radio, but the notion of 'branded content' takes the idea a step further – instead of just financing the programme, the advertiser actually creates the programme. The result is essentially a fusion of an ad and a TV show.

In the 1930s, companies such as Procter & Gamble sponsored first radio and then TV dramas aimed at women, to help sell their cleaning products – the original 'soap operas'. But the shows were not about cleaning; P&G still had to rely on the ad-breaks to get their commercial messages across.

In the early twenty-first century, with consumers exposed to more commercials than ever, and TiVo making the adverts skippable (see **No. 89, TiVo**), marketers began to explore ways of putting their message into the programme itself.

In 2001, BMW created a hugely ambitious project – a series of short films called *The Hire*, shot by some of the world's leading directors, including Ang Lee, Tony Scott, Guy Ritchie and John Woo. They featured big-name actors, such as Mickey Rourke and Gary Oldman, and although each of their plots was different, Clive Owen starred in every film, playing a mysterious character known as 'The Driver', who had a penchant for BMW sports cars. No money was spent on buying TV airtime – the films were released on DVD and on the internet, and achieved a staggering 100 million views. The project kick-started a branded content boom, with marketers including Unilever, Gillette, Adidas and Vodafone subsequently producing their own TV shows.

One advantage of creating their own programme rather than spon- soring a pre-existing property is that marketers are able to craft the content so it showcases their product in the best possible light – for example, *The Hire* was jam-packed with car chases. And by integrating their product into a longer-form piece of film, advertisers feel they are engaging consumers on a deeper level than they could with an ad. *The Hire* also proved that branded content does not even need to be shown on TV, it can be released purely online and if it is entertaining enough, it will attract an audience. ∎

*The breakthrough interactive ad, Crispin Porter & Bogusky's 'Subservient Chicken' for Burger King (2001), in which visitors to a website could type instructions (e.g. 'flap your wings' or 'bend over') to a man dressed in a chicken suit. The tagline was 'Chicken just the way you like it.'*

"'Involve me and I'll understand.'"

*Ads you can play with*

IDEA № 94
# INTERACTIVE ADVERTISING

For centuries, companies sent out advertising messages that the public would either notice, or ignore. But in the mid-1990s, new digital technology enabled the creation of advertising that consumers could affect and change. For the first time, consumers were not just looking at ads, they were playing with them.

*ABOVE: This 2009 interactive video campaign by Abbott Mead Vickers BBDO for London's Metropolitan Police anti-knife crime initiative consisted of a series of linked YouTube films, each of which ended with a choice ... and consequences.*

*BELOW: In 2011, Lynx let consumers 'interact with angels', via augmented reality technology, in London's Victoria Station.*

A typical interactive ad might be an online banner with an intriguing image and a headline that encourages the consumer to click, drag something, or mouse over it – usually because it looks like fun, occasionally with the promise of a reward, or often just 'to see what happens'.

As technology evolves, advertisers have invented numerous innovative and creative ways to cajole users into interaction: Axe turned web-surfers' cursors into a feather they could use to tickle an attractive woman; GE asked consumers to type 'two words' into a banner representing the two biggest challenges facing our future; and hair-care brand Wella let users blow models' hair around by blowing into their computer's microphone. It is now common for ad agencies to create brand micro-sites that are effectively 'digital playgrounds', with content that web users can alter, tailor or re-mix.

Interactivity is also increasingly being seen out-of-home, in the form of digital billboards that people can interact with via their smartphones. (See also **No. 80, Mobile**.)

Building interactivity can be expensive for advertisers, because the technology involved is more complex than for traditional media executions, but it is seen as a value-adding feature, since a user who interacts with an ad will experience a higher degree of engagement with the advertiser's message than someone who has merely viewed it. To quote an old proverb: 'Tell me and I'll forget; show me and I may remember; involve me and I'll understand.' ∎

# The social network

IDEA № 95

# FACEBOOK

Facebook is a social-networking site, launched in 2004, where users can create a profile, add other users as friends and share messages, photos, videos and event invitations. Named after the class lists handed out by universities in the US, it is the world's second most popular website (after Google).

Facebook created the first real opportunity for brands to have an open and continuing dialogue with consumers. If marketers can entice the site's users into 'liking' their page – and brands such as Red Bull, Disney, Starbucks and Coca-Cola have over *20 million* fans on Facebook – they can then send them news and announcements, or ask them for their ideas and suggestions, all for free.

Marketers today are striving to make their fans 'active' by presenting them with questions, photos and video clips that will cause them to leave a comment or click the 'like' button, since not only does each interaction create a deeper engagement between consumer and brand, but it is also transmitted to all of that user's friends, via Facebook's notification system.

It is this feature that has also driven a huge growth in Facebook apps and competitions, which for mainstream brands have begun to supersede Facebook's relatively ineffective display ads.

They take the 'viral effect' to a whole new level, since an entertaining app or contest does not just spread from individual to individual, as is the case when someone forwards an email to a friend, but between entire groups of friends, potentially reaching millions. Marketers obviously have to pay for the creation of these 'social objects', and usually invest in banner ads to promote them, but the successful ones will then spread throughout Facebook under their own steam, providing a phenomenal return on investment (see also **No.84, Viral Marketing** and **No.85, Social Media**). ∎

# Bigger than television

*BOTTOM LEFT: YouTube now sells commercials that play automatically before selected videos. To avoid alienating viewers, the site has begun making most of these 'pre-roll' ads skippable.*

IDEA № 96
## YOUTUBE

YouTube is a video-sharing website whose scale is beginning to dwarf that of television. Most of the site's material is user-generated, but increasingly it is hosting professionally created content such as music videos, TV shows – and ads.

YouTube launched in 2005, and by the time of only its fifth birthday in 2010 it was reporting 'nearly double the prime-time audience of all three major US television networks combined'. Its strength is depth of content – more video is uploaded to YouTube in one month than the three major US networks created in 60 years. As of 2012, YouTube's users are uploading one hour of video every second, and watching a staggering 4 billion videos a day.

Naturally, this is an un-ignorable audience for advertisers; 98 of *Ad Age*'s Top 100 advertisers have already run campaigns on YouTube. Aside from the site's sheer scale, YouTube offers the attractive ability to target very precise demographics and interest groups; for example, a cosmetics brand could buy advertising in and around make-up tutorial videos. It also gives advertisers the opportunity to produce interactive creative ideas, or have viewers click straight through to related videos – features that TV cannot offer.

But YouTube has also created a phenomenon that could be the Holy Grail for advertisers: viewers actively seeking out commercials, or sharing them with their friends. For example, Volkswagen's 2012 Super Bowl spot 'The Force' has been viewed over 53 million times on the platform – for free. (The cost of reaching so many viewers on television would be immense.) Increasingly, an ad's 'shareability' is becoming an important consideration for marketers, since every share is a free view.

YouTube's growing popularity has even changed the way advertisers launch their TV commercials. Previously, marketers kept their Super Bowl spots strictly under wraps until they were broadcast during the game. But Volkswagen uploaded 'The Force' on to YouTube two whole weeks before it aired during the Super Bowl, and scored over 10 million views before the game even began. ∎

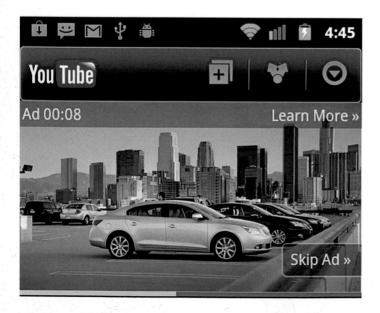

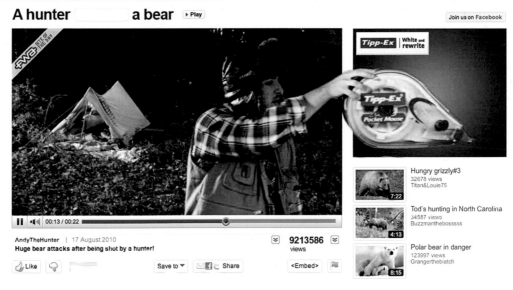

A hunter ⬜⬜⬜⬜ a bear  ▶ Play

Join us on Facebook

Tipp-Ex | White and rewrite

FWA SITE OF THE DAY

Tipp-Ex Pocket Mouse

⏸ 🔊 00:13 / 00:22

AndyTheHunter  |  17 August 2010
Huge bear attacks after being shot by a hunter!

9213586
views

👍 Like  👎  ▢▢▢  Save to ▾  ✉📘 Share  <Embed> 🚩

Hungry grizzly#3
32678 views
Titan&Louie75
7:22

Tod's hunting in North Carolina
34587 views
Buzzmanthebosssss
4:13

Polar bear in danger
123997 views
Grangerthebiatch
8:15

'Every share is a free view.'

# Ads made by Joe Public

IDEA № 97

# USER-GENERATED CONTENT

With high-quality digital video cameras now easily affordable, you do not need the backing of a Hollywood studio to make a film – and you do not need an advertising agency to make an ad. Marketers as diverse as Nestle, L'Oréal and General Mills have invited consumers themselves to create some of their commercials, as opposed to an ad agency.

One of the earliest examples of user-generated ads dates from 2005, when two men in lab coats began dropping Mentos into bottles of Diet Coke and filming the results. The films were an internet sensation and prompted Mentos to sponsor the pair's later efforts. In 2006, Doritos began crowdsourcing their Super Bowl commercials; several other firms have since followed. Usually the ads are sourced via a competition hosted on Facebook, or the company's website. The winner is then either selected by the company, or chosen by public vote.

The cost of the finished product is said to be 60 per cent lower than advertising produced via the traditional ad agency model, so it is certainly a threat to that model. In 2009, the top-selling German newspaper *Bild* had so much success with crowdsourcing its advertising that the paper is now offering user-generated advertising as a service to its advertisers – bypassing the ad agencies completely.

Arguably, crowdsourcing works best for straightforward, well-established campaigns, whereas more strategically challenging campaigns or complex brand repositioning exercises still require a collaboration between advertiser and advertising agency. And since user-generated content is outside the company's direct control, it has to be carefully managed, perhaps even pre-vetted.

When Chevrolet put a tool on its website that allowed visitors to create their own commercial for its Tahoe sport utility vehicle (SUV), the feature was hijacked by anti-SUV activists who made videos criticizing the vehicle's poor fuel efficiency and its negative impact on the environment. ∎

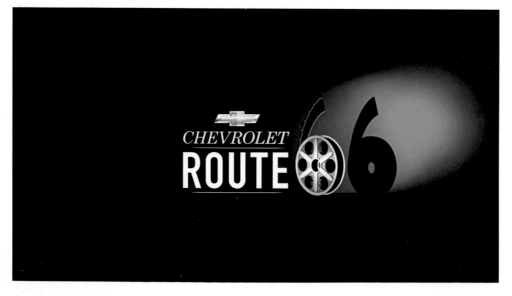

TOP RIGHT: *Crowdsourced ad for Peperami Nibblers, 2010. The winning entry came from a freelance creative team, leading some to argue this was cut-price creative outsourcing rather than true user-generated content.*

LEFT: *Chevrolet hired a company called MOFILM, which specialises in sourcing user-generated content, to run a competition to create its 2012 Super Bowl commercial.*

'You do not need an advertising agency to make an ad.'

ABOVE: Doritos' crowdsourced ads have proved extremely popular – the 2008 Super Bowl commercial was ranked by USA Today as the No.1 ad of the year and earned its creators a $1 million prize

# Selling in 140 characters or less

IDEA № 98
# TWITTER

Twitter is a social networking platform that enables users to send and read short text-based posts known as tweets. Its rapid growth and uniquely 'social' environment have made it an in-demand new channel for advertisers.

Twitter launched in July 2006 and quickly shot to worldwide popularity, reaching 300 million users by 2011. In 2012, even the Pope sent his first tweet.

The site began accepting advertising in 2010 in the form of 'promoted tweets', which appear in a user's Twitter stream and whose content relates to tweets the user is reading or searching for. Today they are rumoured to cost $100,000 a pop; however, the rate at which they trigger a consumer interaction – at around 3 to 5 per cent – is much higher than for other forms of online advertising, such as banners. Promoted tweets were quickly followed by further innovations such as 'promoted trends' and 'promoted accounts'.

Despite the predictions of some naysayers, consumers seem to have accepted the appearance of advertising on Twitter, since they understand that media owners have the right to profit from their popularity, especially if ad revenues (as is the case with Twitter) enable the service to be provided free of charge. But advertisers have found there is an important sense in which social media differs from 'traditional' media; social media is a conversation and crass attempts to 'push' corporate messaging usually fall flat.

In 2012, Qantas faced a backlash in Australia when it launched a competition offering Twitter users the chance to win a trivial-sounding 'luxury amenity kit', including its 'famous PJs', at a time when customers were angry because the airline's fleet had been grounded due to industrial action. And when McDonald's purchased the trend #McDStories hoping that Twitter users would share tales of burger-related happiness, it was not prepared to see the hashtag overwhelmed by stories about diabetes, obesity and alleged genetic-engineering of McNuggets. ∎

TWELP FORCE — TWITTER.COM/TWELPFORCE

america

twitter

Home Profile Find People Settings Help Sign out

## Toronto we're here! 1st 500 click http://bit.ly/TorVX to score a #VXREDHOT promo code to fly w/a friend for 50% off+WiFi. See fare rules

about 2 hours ago via web
Retweeted by 12 people

Reply  Retweet

**VirginAmerica**
Virgin America

© 2010 Twitter  About Us  Contact  Blog  Status  Goodies  API  Business  Help  Jobs  Terms  Privacy

FLYDEALISTS UNITE!

## Search results for **starbucks**

Save this search

**Starbucks** On 4/15 bring in a reusable tumbler and we'll fill it with brewed coffee for free. Let's all switch from paper cups. http://bit.ly/9ZDP6N

about 8 hours ago via CoTweet by bradnelson
Promoted by Starbucks Coffee  100+ Retweets

'Social media is a conversation, and crass attempts to "push" corporate messaging usually fall flat.'

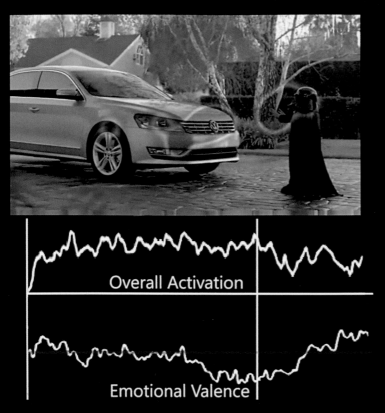

Overall Activation

Emotional Valence

'A decision based on science.'

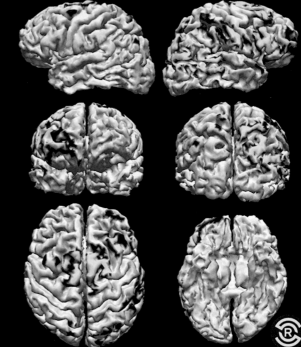

# *Inside consumers' brains*

IDEA № 99
# NEUROMARKETING

New findings about how the brain works are starting to have an impact on how advertising is created. A new wave of research companies have begun using neuroscientific technology – originally developed for medical purposes – to scan consumers' brains. And marketers are using the information to refine their advertising messages.

The practice began in about 2006, is growing rapidly, and has been employed by brands as mainstream as McDonald's, Unilever and Volkswagen.

For decades, advertisers have used research groups to ask consumers what they think of an advertisement. But people in research groups may lie, or their feedback may be skewed because they are sitting in the artificial environment of a research group, or they may simply not have access to their real responses – over 90 per cent of what humans think and feel takes place at a level below conscious awareness.

Neuromarketing is a research technique that aims to find out what people are really thinking and feeling when they watch an ad, by using electroencephalography (EEG) and functional magnetic resonance imaging (fMRI) to see what is going on in their brains. The claim is that this information can help clients develop advertising that will be more appealing and hence drive more sales.

Using a brain scan, researchers can certainly read with great accuracy how well an ad is grabbing a viewer's attention and whether it engages them emotionally. Neuroscience can even determine which images in an ad are having an effect on the brain's reward system – thus making the consumer more likely to buy. In this way, low-scoring ads can either be altered to make them more effective, or scrapped entirely, enabling the client to avoid spending millions on an ineffective piece of communication.

Results are still somewhat speculative and open to interpretation. But the current excitement around neuroscience is that it could one day bring a degree of certainty to the art of persuasion, and that rather than having to commit to a commercial based on a combination of 'gut feel' and a slick presentation from their ad agency, it will enable marketers to make a decision based on science. ∎

## The power of a nudge

IDEA № 100
# BEHAVIOURAL ECONOMICS

Behavioural economics is a new academic discipline that studies how people make decisions. Its central claim is that our choices are not wholly rational and we are heavily influenced by how choices are *presented*. The interest for advertisers is obvious: behavioural economics suggests powerful new persuasion techniques.

ABOVE: *A smiley face for drivers who obey the speed limit, a frowning face for speeders. 10 per cent of the cost of a speed camera and prevents twice as many accidents.*

It was the publication of *Nudge: Improving Decisions about Health, Wealth and Happiness* by Richard Thaler and Cass Sunstein in 2008 that brought behavioural economics into public consciousness. The book points out that we make a whole litany of irrational judgements, such as favouring the pleasure that we get from smoking today over the health issues we know it will cause in the future (recency bias), or failing to cancel a subscription to a magazine we do not actually read when the 'first year free' period comes to an end (status quo bias).

Since ad agencies have long argued that we buy products for non-rational reasons – for example, we may buy emotionally, habitually, because others buy something, or because we want to impress others – the book was enthusiastically received in advertising circles and is starting to have an influence on ad campaigns worldwide

*Nudge* draws heavily on behavioural economics to conclude that the most effective way to change behaviour is by careful design of the 'choice architecture' of a decision, in order to 'nudge' rather than coerce people towards a desired outcome. In advertising terms, the implication is that a clever way of presenting the purchasing decision to consumers may be even more effective than advertising the actual attributes of a product or service.

Whereas previously agencies and marketers usually focused on changing consumers' perceptions of a product, the great appeal of 'nudge' thinking is that it may generate ideas that directly change behaviour, rather than just perceptions. ∎

"'Nudge' thinking ... may generate ideas that directly change behaviour.'

*ABOVE: Supermarkets 'nudge' us into believing that everything in the store is healthy, by positioning their fresh produce at the entrance.*

*LEFT: 'Piano Staircase' from VW Sweden for their environmentally conscious Blue Motion series. It showed that people can be persuaded to take the environmentally efficient option, if it is fun.*

# Further Reading

IDEA NO.1 THE POSTER
Paul Rennie, *Modern British Posters: Art, Design & Communication*, 2010
Alain Weill, *Graphics: A Century of Poster and Advertising Design*, 2004

IDEA NO.2 PROMOTIONS
Julian Cummins, Roddy Mullin, *Sales Promotion: How to Create, Implement and Integrate Campaigns that Really Work*, 2010

IDEA NO.3 BRANDING
Rita Clifton, *Brands and Branding*, 2009

IDEA NO.4 THE LEAFLET
Nicola Ackland-Snow, Nathan Brett, Steven Williams, *Fly: The Art of the Club Flyer*, 1997

IDEA NO.7 APPROPRIATION
Barry Hoffman, *The Fine Art of Advertising*, 2003

IDEA NO.9 PUBLICITY STUNTS
Al Ries, Laura Ries, *The Fall of Advertising and the Rise of PR*, 2004

IDEA NO.12 SEX IN ADVERTISING
Tom Reichert, *The Erotic History of Advertising*, 2003
Juliann Sivulka, *Sex, Soap and Cigarettes*, 1997

IDEA NO.14 PRODUCT PLACEMENT
Kerry Segrave, *Product Placement in Hollywood Films: A History*, 2004.

IDEA NO.16 SLOGANS
Lionel Salem, *Handbook of Slogans*, 2012

IDEA NO.21 CREATIVES
Andrew Cracknell, *The Real Mad Men: The Remarkable True Story of Madison Avenue's Golden Age*, 2011

IDEA NO.23 THE AGENCY AS BRAND
KesselsKramer, *The Worst Hotel in the World: The Hans Brinker Budget Hotel Amsterdam*, 2009

IDEA NO.24 CELEBRITY ENDORSEMENT
George Lois, *$ellebrity: My Angling and Tangling with Famous People*, 2003
Hamish Pringle, *Celebrity Sells*, 2004

IDEA NO.26 DIRECT MAIL
Drayton Bird, *Commonsense Direct and Digital Marketing*, 2007

IDEA NO.28 WOMEN IN THE WORKPLACE
Jane Maas, *Mad Women*, 2012

IDEA NO.29 RADIO
Jim Cox, *Sold on Radio: Advertisers in the Golden Age of Broadcasting*, 2008

IDEA NO.30 SPONSORSHIP
Pippa Collett, William Fenton, *The Sponsorship Handbook: Essential Tools, Tips and Techniques for Sponsors and Sponsorship Seekers*, 2011

IDEA NO.31 SURREALISM
Barry Hoffman, *The Fine Art of Advertising*, 2003

IDEA NO.33 THE JINGLE
Steve Karmen, *Who Killed the Jingle?: How a Unique American Art Form Disappeared*, 2004

IDEA NO.36 TELEVISION ADVERTISING
Brian Henry, *British Television Advertising: The First 30 Years*, 1986
Lawrence R. Samuel, *Brought to You by: Postwar Television Advertising and the American Dream*, 2002

IDEA NO.37 RESEARCH
Joel J. Davis, *Advertising Research: Theory & Practice*, 2011

IDEA NO.38 THE USP
Rosser Reeves, *Reality in Advertising*, 1961

IDEA NO.39 THE INFOMERCIAL
Lou Harry, Sam Stall, *As Seen on TV*, 2002

IDEA NO.40 GRAPHIC DESIGN
Steven Heller, Veronique Vienne, *100 Ideas that Changed Graphic Design*, 2012
Adrian Shaughnessy, *How to be a Graphic Designer, without Losing your Soul*, 2010
Drew de Soto, *Know your Onions: Graphic Design*, 2012

IDEA NO.41 THE BRAINSTORM
Dave Gray, Sunni Brown, James Macanufo, *Gamestorming: A Playbook for Innovators, Rulebreakers, and Changemakers*, 2010
Alex Osborn, *How To Think Up*, 1942

IDEA NO.43 THE PERSONAL BRAND
David Ogilvy, *Ogilvy on Advertising*, 1963

IDEA NO.45 THE CREATIVE REVOLUTION
Bob Levenson, *Bill Bernbach's Book*, 1988

IDEA NO.46 HUMOUR
Charles S. Gulas, Marc G. Weinberger, *Humor in Advertising: A Comprehensive Analysis*, 2006

IDEA NO.47 THE CHALLENGER BRAND
Adam Morgan, *Eating the Big Fish: How Challenger Brands can Compete against Brand Leaders*, 2009

IDEA NO.49 BRAND PERSONALITY THEORY
Joshua C. Chen, Margaret Hartwell, *Archetypes in Branding: A Toolkit for Creatives and Strategists*, 2012

IDEA NO.50 THE POLITICAL ATTACK AD
Brian McNair, *An Introduction to Political Communication*, 2011

IDEA NO.53 DEMOCRATIZATION
Jerry Della Femina, *From those Wonderful Folks who Gave you Pearl Harbor: Front Line Dispatches from the Advertising War*, 1970

IDEA NO.55 ACCOUNT PLANNING
Jon Steel, *Tuth, Lies, and Advertising: The Art of Account Planning*, 1998

IDEA NO.56 SUPERSTAR DIRECTORS
Thomas Richter, *The 30-Second Storyteller: The Art and Business of Directing Commercials*, 2006

IDEA NO.57 POP MUSIC IN ADS
Timothy Taylor, *The Sounds of Capitalism: Advertising, Music, and the Conquest of Culture*, 2012

IDEA NO.60 THE ESP
Marc Gobé, *Emotional Branding: A New Paradigm for Connecting Brands to People*, 2001

IDEA NO.62 THE EVENT AD
Bernice Kanner, *Super Bowl of Advertising: How the Commercials Won the Game*, 2003

IDEA NO.63 WORD OF MOUTH
Mark Hughes, *Buzzmarketing: Get People to Talk about your Stuff*, 2005

IDEA NO.64 NOT ADVERTISING
Ben R. Cohen, Jerry Greenfield, *Ben and Jerry's Double-dip: Lead with your Values and Make Money too*, 1999

Anita Roddick, *Business as Unusual: My Entrepreneurial Journey – Profits with Principles*, 2005

IDEA NO.65 SEMIOTICS
Ron Beasley, Marcel Danesi, *Persuasive Signs: The Semiotics of Advertising*, 2002

IDEA NO.67 ADVERTISING AS FICTION
Peter Carey, *Bliss*, 1981
Samuel Hopkins Adams, *The Clarion*, 1914
Harold Livingston, *The Detroiters*, 1958
Peter Mayle, *A Year in Provence*, 1989
Shepherd Mead, *The Admen*, 1958
George Orwell, *Keep the Aspidistra Flying*, 1936
Harford Powel, *The Virgin Queens*, 1928
Dorothy L. Sayers, *Murder must Advertise*, 1933
Frederic Wakeman, *The Hucksters*, 1946
Sloan Wilson, *The Man in the Gray Flannel Suit*, 1955

IDEA NO.68 ANTI-CAPITALISM
Naomi Klein, *No Logo*, 2000

IDEA NO.70 TRADE ADS
Scot McKee, *Creative B2B Branding (No Really): Building a Creative Brand in a Business World*, 2010

IDEA NO.74 THE MICRO-NETWORK
John Hegarty, *Hegarty on Advertising*, 2011

IDEA NO.75 THE RISE OF THE VISUAL
Paul Messaris, *Visual Persuasion: The Role of Images in Advertising*, 1997

IDEA NO.77 POSTMODERNISM
Stephen Brown, *Postmodern Marketing*, 1995

IDEA NO.79 AMBIENT
Gavin Lucas, Mike Dorrian, *Guerrilla Advertising: Unconventional Brand Communication*, 2006

IDEA NO.81 CRM MARKETING
Roger J. Baran, Robert Galka, *CRM: The Foundation of Contemporary Marketing Strategy*, 2012
Ernan Roman, *Voice-of-the-Customer Marketing: A Proven 5-Step Process to Create Customers who Care, Spend, and Stay*, 2010

IDEA NO.83 OPEN PLAN
Franklin Becker PhD, William Sims PhD, *Offices that Work*, 2001 (http://iwsp.human.cornell.edu)
Tom de Marco, Timothy Lister, *Peopleware*, 1987

IDEA NO.84 VIRAL MARKETING
Justin Kirby, Paul Marsden, *Connected Marketing: The Viral, Buzz and Word of Mouth Revolution*, 2005
Richard Perry, Andrew Whittaker, *Understanding Viral Marketing in a Week*, 2002

IDEA NO.85 SOCIAL MEDIA
Guy Clapperton, *This is Social Media: Tweet, Blog, Link and Post your Way to Business Success*, 2009
Christopher Locke, Doc Searls, David Weinberger, *The Cluetrain Manifesto*, 2000

IDEA NO.86 ONLINE ADVERTISING
Daniele Fiandaca, Patrick Burgoyne, *Digital Advertising: Past, Present, and Future*, 2010

IDEA NO.87 DECLINE OF THE COMMISSION SYSTEM
W. J. Reilly, *Effects of the Advertising Agency Commission System*, 1931

IDEA NO.88 THE DOT-COM BOOM
Ernst Malmsten, *Boo Hoo: A dot.com Story from Concept to Catastrophe*, 2001
Roger Lowenstein, *Origins of the Crash: The Great Bubble and its Undoing*, 2004

IDEA NO.90 SEARCH
Brad Geddes, *Advanced Google AdWords*, 2012
Steven Levy, *In the Plex: How Google Thinks, Works and Shapes our Lives*, 2011
Jon Smith, *Google Adwords that Work: 7 Secrets to Cashing in with the No.1 Search Engine*, 2008

IDEA NO.92 ADVERGAMES
Jason Fincanon, *Flash Advertising: Flash Platform Development of Microsites, Advergames and Branded Applications*, 2010

IDEA NO.93 BRANDED CONTENT
Norton Fau Garfield, *Branded Content*, 2011

IDEA NO.94 INTERACTIVE ADVERTISING
*One Club, One Show Interactive: Advertising's Best Interactive & New Media*, annual
Joe Plummer, Stephen D. Rappaport, Taddy Hall, Robert Barocci, *The Online Advertising Playbook: Proven Strategies and Tested Tactics from the Advertising Research Foundation*, 2007

IDEA NO.95 FACEBOOK
Ben Mezrich, *The Accidental Billionaires: The Founding of Facebook, a Tale of Sex, Money, Genius, and Betrayal*, 2009
Perry Marshall, Thomas Meloche, *Ultimate Guide to Facebook Advertising: How to Access 600 Million Customers in 10 Minutes*, 2011

IDEA NO.97 USER-GENERATED CONTENT
http://www.mofilm.com/

IDEA NO.98 TWITTER
Eileen Brown, *Working the Crowd: Social Media Marketing for Business*, 2010

IDEA NO.99 NEUROMARKETING
Erik du Plessis, *The Branded Mind: What Neuroscience really Tells us about the Puzzle of the Brain and the Brand*, 2011
Leon Zurawicki, *Neuromarketing: Exploring the Brain of the Consumer*, 2010

IDEA NO.100 BEHAVIOURAL ECONOMICS
Dan Ariely, *Predictably Irrational*, 2009
Barry Schwartz, *The Paradox of Choice*, 2005
Richard Thaler, Cass Sunstein, *Nudge: Improving Decisions about Health, Wealth, and Happiness*, 2008

# Index

# Index

# Index

# Picture Credits

2: Jiri Rezac / Alamy. 8b: Tony Lilley / Alamy. 9: Historical Picture Archive/CORBIS. 10t: Image courtesy of Eurostar. 11: Image Courtesy of The Advertising Archives.12: Peter Worth / Alamy. 13t: Courtesy of AB InBev UK Limited. 13b: ADVERTISING AGENCY: RKCR/Y&R LONDON, ART DIRECTOR: TIM BROOKES, COPYWRITER: PHIL FORSTER, ILLUSTRATOR: LEE ALDRIDGE, CLIENT: LAND ROVER. 14t: Image courtesy of Charles E. Snyder. 14b: Image courtesy of the Environment Agency, Abu Dhabi. 15: Illustrator: Matthias Tratz.16t: Agency: Young & Rubicam Paris. 3D artist: Patrick Gernigon. 16b: North Wind Picture Archives. 17: Hulton Archive/Getty Images. 20: Client: American Honda Motor Co., Inc. Client Name: Michael Accavitti, SVP, Automobile Operarions American Honda Motor Co., Inc. Ad agnecy: RPA. Chief Creative Officer: Joe Baratelli, EVP. Executive Creative Director: Jason Sperling, SVP. Creative Directors: Chuck Blackwell VP, Ken Pappanduros VP. Art Director: Ariel Shukert. Sr Copyrighter: David Sullivan. Executive Producer, Content: Gary Paticoff, SVP. Executive Producer: Isadora Chesler, VP. Director of Business Affairs: Maria Del Homme, VP. Production company: Moxie Pictures. Editorial company: Union Editorial. VFX/Telecine company: The Mill. Music company: Beacon Street Studios. 21l: Smithsonian Institution, Arthur M. Sackler Gallery, The Anne van Biema Collection / The Bridgeman Art Library. 21r: Peter Harholdt/CORBIS. 23t: Olycom SPA/REX. 24t: REX/Solent News. 24b: Agency: Duval Guillaume Modem. Client Director: Igor Nowé, Bart Geemers. Creative Directors: Geoffrey Hantson. Creative team: Koenraad Lefever, Katrien Bottez, Dries DeWilde. Account Director: Elke Janssens. Production Company: Monodot, Brussels. Director: Cecilia Verheyden Producer: Tatjana Pierre. 25: Oli Scarff/Staff/Getty Images News. 26: Stacy Walsh Rosenstock / Alamy. 27t: Bettmann/CORBIS. 27b: Image Courtesy of The Advertising Archives. 28b: Archive Photos/Getty Images. 29: Image courtesy of Ford. 30–31: Wong Maye-E/AP/Press Association Images. 30: Image Courtesy of The Advertising Archives. 31: Image Courtesy of The Advertising Archives. 32b: Time & Life Pictures/Getty Images. 34t: REX / ©Paramount/Everett. 34b: REX/©20thC. Fox/Everett. 35: REX/Snap Stills. 36t: Archive Photos/Getty Images. 37: John Chapple/Hulton Archive/Getty Images. 38-39: Jiri Rezac / Alamy. 40: REX/Nils Jorgensen. 44: REX/ Everett Collection. 45t:Image Courtesy of The Advertising Archives. 45b: Image Courtesy of The Advertising Archives. 47 middle-right: AFP/Getty Images. 48t: Courtesy of Ogilvy & Mather UK. 48b: Condé Nast Archive/Corbis. 49: Image Courtesy of The Advertising Archives. 49: Image Courtesy of The Advertising Archives. 49:Image Courtesy of The Advertising Archives. 52b: www.motherlondon. com. 54: Image courtesy of Abbott Mead Vickers BBDO. 55t: REX/C Bush / Everett. 55b: Jeremy Sutton-Hibbert / Alamy. 56: Swim Ink 2, LLC/CORBIS.57t:Image courtesy of PETA www.peta.org. 57b: Image courtesy of California Department of Public Health. 58t: Creative Director: Clinton Manson, Dominic Stallard. Copywriter: Clinton Manson. Art Director: Dominic Stallard 59t: Agency: Cossette, Toronto. 60t: Shutterstock. 60b: Gilles Mingasson /Hulton Archive/Getty Images. 61b:Thomas Barwick/Getty. 62t: Image Courtesy of The Advertising Archives. 64t: AF archive / Alamy. 64b: Getty Images.65: Image Courtesy of The Advertising Archives. 66-67: Clive Mason/Getty Images. 66b: John Gichigi/Hulton Archive/Getty Images. 67: Image Courtesy of The Advertising Archives. 68-69: © MOURON. CASSANDRE. Lic 2014-26-01-01 www.cassandre.fr. 68b: Image courtesy of David Hughes. 70: Image courtesy of

PETA www.peta.org. 71l: Jeff Greenberg "0 people images" / Alamy. 71r: Image Courtesy of The Advertising Archives. 72: Photo courtesy of McDonald's Corporation.73: Sound Mark is a trademark of Intel Corporation in the U.S. and/or other countries. 74–75: Image courtesy of Procter & Gamble. 76t: Iconographic Collection, J. Walter Thompson Co. archives, David M. Rubenstein Rare Book & Manuscript Library, Duke University. 76b: ©UNITED ARTISTS. 77: AMC / THE KOBAL COLLECTION. 80: Courtesy of Fallon. 81r: Image courtesy of Ford. 81l: Image Courtesy of The Advertising Archives. 86: Courtesy of George Lois. 89: Images courtesy of the author. 92b: Image courtesy of Beattie McGuinness Bungay. 93: Bettmann/ CORBIS. 94-95: David Speck/Demotix/Corbis. 98: Agency: Leo Burnett London. Writer: Paul Silburn. Art director: Paul Silburn. Director: Danny Kleinman. Production company: Spectre. 102t: Courtesy: National Highway Traffic Safety Administration. 104: Used with permission from Microsoft.105b: Image courtesy of BAV Consulting. 108: Courtesy of Exxon Mobil Corporation. 109t: Image courtesy of Deutsch. 110t: Michael Neelon / Alamy. 110b: Courtesy of BETC. 111: The Granger Collection / TopFoto. 13b: Birds Eye® is a registered trademark of Pinnacle Foods Group LLC. Image Courtesy of The Advertising Archives. 115: AMC / THE KOBAL COLLECTION. 117: Image Courtesy of The Advertising Archives. 119: Image Courtesy of The Advertising Archives. 120: STEFF/CORBIS. 121: ASSOCIATED PRESS/Paul Sakuma. 122: Courtesy of VW and Paula Hamilton. 123t: Unilever. 123b: © TAO Images Limited / Alamy. 125: Getty Images. 126t: Image courtesy of Patek Philippe. Photographer: Peggy Sirota, model Ed Locke (father). 127: REX/Brendan Beirne. 128: Kathy deWitt / Alamy. 129t: Courtesy of AB InBev UK Limited. 129b: Image Courtesy of The Advertising Archives. 130-131: Agency: Adam &Eve DDB. Model: Lewis McGowan from Superior Model Management
132b: Illustration by Tom Fishburne. 133: Bloomberg/ Getty Images. 134t: WireImage/Getty. 135b: Courtesy of Wieden+Kennedy. 135: John Lamm/Transtock/Corbis. 136:Image Courtesy of The Advertising Archives. 137t: ABSOLUT® VODKA. ABSOLUT COUNTRY OF SWEDEN VODKA & LOGO, ABSOLUT, ABSOLUT BOTTLE DESIGN AND ABSOLUT CALLIGRAPHY ARE TRADEMARKS OWNED BY THE ABSOLUT COMPANY AB. 137b:Ad agency: Young & Rubicam, Paris. 138t: Courtesy of Haymarket. 140: REX/ Moviestore Collection. 141l: Photos 12 / Alamy. 141r: AF archive / Alamy. 142t: Courtesy of Adbusters Media Foundation. 143: Scott Houston/Corbis. 146t: Vancouver Convention Center. Photography: Anthony Redpath. Agency: DDB Canada. 148t: Jason Morgan / Daily Billboard Blog. 148b: Courtesy of Lloyds Banking Group. 149: Image Courtesy of The Advertising Archives. 150–151: iStock. 150b: ©2013 Destination Media, Inc. 152: Craig Spivey Concept, Copy and Art Direction. Photograph of Bob Marley by Dennis Morris. Account Director Jeremy Eaton. 153t: Campaign: Diarr ER Creators: Asa Rodger & Andy Wainwright. Company: Fifth Ring Ltd. 153b: Courtesy of C21. Neil Parsons – Senior Designer. Shane Haddock Creative Director. 154: Photo: Hans Gissinger. 156t: ©2014. The LEGO Group, used with permission. 156b: Agency: Jung von Matt, Hamburg, Germany. Creative Director: Arno Lindemann, Bernhard Lukas. Copywriter: Daniel Schaefer. Art Director: Szymon Rose. Photographer: Achim Lippoth. 157:Agency: Jung von Matt, Hamburg, Germany. Creative-GF: Deneke von Weltzien. Art Director: Reza Ramezani Text / Concept: Johannes Milhofer. 158:

Courtesy of Unilever. 159: Executive Director: Rémi Babinet, Art Director: Agnés Cavard, Copyrighter: Valerie Chidlovsky, Assistan Art Director: Gregory Ferembach, TV Producer: Fabrice Brovelli, Music Supervisor: Christophe Caurret, Music: BETC Music, Production House: Partizan, Director: Michael Gracey. 160: Image Courtesy of The Advertising Archives. 163: Images courtesy of the author. 166t: Advertising Agency: Beattie McGuinness Bungay London. Art Director: Dom Martin. Technology Lead: Toby De Havilland. Flash Designer: Carl Loodberg. Action Scripter: Andreas Alptun. Creative Lead (Digital) Martin Buckwell. Account Director: Clare Campbell. Account Manager: Dylan Davenport. Account Executive: Sonia Friel. 168: Newscast / Alamy. 169t: Copywriter: Nicky Bullard (now executive creative director) Art director: Tim Styles. Designers: Marek Charytonowicz, Dan Newman, Technical Director: Jon Chandler Deputy Planning Director: Ben Parr Account Director: Clare Willetts External organisations: New Moon – Post production Molinaire – Animation. 169b: Image courtesy of Procter & Gamble. 172: Designer Mathieu Lehanneur. Architect: Ana Moussinet. 173t: www.motherlondon.com. 173b: Image ©Joost Vianen. 175b: Image Courtesy of The Advertising Archives. 176t: © Invisible Children is a 501©(3) non-profit that exists to bring a permanent end to LRA atrocities. www.invisiblechildren.com 176b: © Moviestore collection Ltd / Alamy. 177: Courtesy of Wieden+Kennedy and Isaiah Mustafa. 179b: Agency: Memac Ogilvy Dubai and OgilvyOne Frankfurt. Client: Sven Markschlaeger - Web Channel Manager, IKEA. Creative Director: Ben Knight, Robin Smith. Art Director: Gary Rolf. Designer: Gary Rolf. Copywriter: Gary Rolf, James Bisset. Technical Directors: Jens Steffen, Niv Baniahmad, Hamza Afaq. Regional Business Director: Claus Adams. Account Manager: Farnoush Pourebrahim. 181t: Image Courtesy of The Advertising Archives. 181b: Photographic Services, Shell International Ltd. Image Courtesy of The Advertising Archives. 182t: Getty Images. 183: Image Courtesy of The Advertising Archives. 184: WARNER BROS. TV / CHUCK LORRE PROD. / THE KOBAL COLLECTION. 185t: Image courtesy of Sainsbury's. 187b: Images courtesy of Jung von Matt/Neckar. 188t: GEORGE WIDMAN/AP/Press Association Imagess. 189: Jamie McDonald/Getty Images. 190b: Image courtesy of Xbox. 193t: Courtesy of McCann Australia. 193b: Photo courtesy of McDonald's Australia Limited. WTFN Entertainment Pty Ltd. 195t: Copywriter: Martin Loraine, Art Director: Steve Jones, Agency Planner: Tom White, Media Agency. MediaCom, Media Planner: Duncan Snowden, Production: Mad Cow Films, Director: Simon Ellis, Production Co.Producer: Pete Chambers, Post-production: The Mill. 195b: Courtesy of Unilever. 196l: Art Director; Matthew Pullen. 197: Images courtesy of Intel. 199t: Forensic Artist Gil Zamora. Sketch-Artist LLC. Model:Kela Cabrales. 199b: Tipp-Ex® Ad is : Buzzman/ BIC ®. 200t: Image Courtesy of The Advertising Archives. 200t: Image Courtesy of The Advertising Archives. 204t: Image courtesy of Sands Research. 204b: BrainBand EEG Headset by MyndPlay. Image from the Measure of Pleasure experiment for Beyond Dark Chocolate and Ogilvy Digital Labs – James Nester & Graham Jenks. BirkBeck University London, Mervyn Etienne – Cognitive Neuroscientist. Tre Azam – CEO MyndPlay. 205: Artwork: Richie Wykes. 206: © Hugh Threlfall / Alamy. 207t: Tina Manley / Alamy. 207b: www.thefuntheory.com.

Published in 2015 by
Laurence King Publishing Ltd
361–373 City Road
London EC1V 1LR

e-mail: enquiries@laurenceking.com
www.laurenceking.com

This book was designed and produced by
Laurence King Publishing Ltd, London.

A catalogue record for this book is available
from the British Library.

ISBN: 978 1 78067 234 2

Book design: Struktur Design
Original series design: TwoSheds Design
Picture research: Evi Peroulaki
Senior editor: John Parton

Printed in China